GROWING ORGANIC FRUIT AND VEGETABLES IN SMALL SPACES:

A Beginners Guide for an Abundant Harvest using Pots, Containers, and Grow Bags

Casey Eden

© Copyright 2024 - All rights reserved.

The content contained within this book may not be reproduced, duplicated or transmitted without direct written permission from the author or the publisher.

Under no circumstances will any blame or legal responsibility be held against the publisher, or author, for any damages, reparation, or monetary loss due to the information contained within this book, either directly or indirectly.

Legal Notice:

This book is copyright protected. It is only for personal use. You cannot amend, distribute, sell, use, quote or paraphrase any part, or the content within this book, without the consent of the author or publisher.

Disclaimer Notice:

Please note the information contained within this document is for educational and entertainment purposes only. All effort has been executed to present accurate, up to date, reliable, complete information. No warranties of any kind are declared or implied. Readers acknowledge that the author is not engaged in the rendering of legal, financial, medical or professional advice. The content within this book has been derived from various sources. Please consult a licensed professional before attempting any techniques outlined in this book.

By reading this document, the reader agrees that under no circumstances is the author responsible for any losses, direct or indirect, that are incurred as a result of the use of the information contained within this document, including, but not limited to, errors, omissions, or inaccuracies.

ISBN: 978-1-7386195-2-8 paperback

ISBN: 978-1-7386195-3-5 ebook

Table of Contents

Introduction

Ah, the magic of tending to your own little patch of green, no matter how small! There's something profoundly satisfying about nurturing life, even in the coziest of spaces that are often wasted or overlooked. Welcome to the world of organic container gardening.

Container gardening is a delightful and accessible way for beginners to cultivate their own green oasis right from the comfort of their homes, balconies, or even tiny urban spaces. It provides an opportunity to nurture plants, grow fresh produce, and surround oneself with nature's beauty, all within the confines of manageable containers.

In this bustling modern age, space comes at a premium. Yet, the desire to cultivate our own fruits and vegetables persists. That's where the enchantment of small-scale organic gardening comes into play. It's like having a mini-oasis right outside your doorstep. Trust me, I've been there. My own little balcony transformed into a vibrant tapestry of greens, thanks to the joys of container gardening.

Now, why go organic, you might wonder? It's not just about avoiding chemicals (although that's a huge plus). It's about embracing a lifestyle that's kinder to our planet and our bodies. When you nurture your plants with organic care, you're not just growing food; you're cultivating a connection with nature, one that pays dividends in both health (physically and mentally) and sustainability.

I grew up in the city. We were a family of city dwellers who couldn't manage to grow flowers, let alone fruit and vegetables (despite the family home having enough land for us to be self-sufficient). I had always wanted to grow my own food, and around the time the COVID-19 pandemic hit in 2020, I looked up what I thought would be great veggies to grow and bought up a raft of plants. I had absolutely no idea what I was doing, so I planted the veggies straight into the soil. Living only a couple of blocks from the beach, the soil was fairly sandy.

Despite the bad start, I have persevered. Viewing this as a steep learning curve, I have kept at it. My motivations are rocketing food and fuel prices, a desire to be self-sufficient (at least that is the goal), and wanting to eat organically. If anyone who couldn't tell the difference between a flower and a weed can grow their own food, then anyone can.

In my first book, *Grow Your Own Vegetables*, I provided a beginner's guide for all things gardening, including in-ground gardens. Now, we will focus on using even the tiniest of spaces to grow your crops.

Our journey together begins by laying the groundwork. We'll dive into the nitty-gritty of soil selection and preparation. You'll learn how to create a thriving ecosystem in those modest containers, ensuring your plants flourish from root to leaf. And, of course, composting, the heart and soul of organic gardening. Even in the tiniest of apartments, there's room for a composting corner, and I'll show you how.

Then, it's time to choose your green companions. We'll explore your limited space's best fruits and vegetables, season by season. Should you start with seeds or opt for young seedlings? Don't fret; we'll tackle that too. And when those pesky critters come a-knocking, fear not! I've got a bag of organic tricks up my sleeve to keep your garden pest-free and thriving.

As we journey on, we will explore every facet of container gardening, from selecting the right containers to choosing the perfect plants for your space. You will discover the secrets of organic fertilization and nutrient management, and you will even learn how to regrow food from kitchen scraps. We will walk through the day-to-day care that keeps your plants happy and healthy right up to the glorious harvest.

By the end of this book, you will have a solid foundation to create your container garden. So, let's embark on this delightful journey of organic container gardening together and turn your limited space into a flourishing, sustainable haven. Dig in and embrace the joy of nurturing life, one leaf at a time!

Helpful Gardening Terms You'll Definitely Want to Know

I remember during one of my first-ever trips to my local nursery for gardening supplies, it felt like the sales assistants spoke a completely different language. They used words that I've never come across and left me so confused that I almost gave up on my dream of growing my own organic crops before I even planted my first seed. Luckily, I didn't!

I realized that to be successful in my gardening journey, I had to expand my overall knowledge of gardening and understand the lingo that avid gardeners (and sales assistants) used. Just like you need healthy soil to grow your crops, you also need a strong foundation of key terms to build your garden on.

For this reason, I want to share some important gardening terminology with you before we even get into the basics of container gardening. Some of these terms you'll see used throughout this book, while others will help to expand your overall gardening knowledge, or IQ, as I like to refer to it.

Annual plant: A plant that goes from start to finish in a single season. This includes germinating from seed, reaching maturity, blooming and producing vegetables, and dying. Examples of annual plants include tomatoes, basil, and lettuce.

Biennials: These plants' life cycle stretches over two seasons. Typically, the plant will produce roots and leaves during the first season. Over the next season, it will bloom and produce vegetables or fruit.

Bolting: When a plant starts to flower and shoots seeds too early, it is bolting. This will typically result in a small harvest, if any.

Companion planting: This is when you purposefully place two plants in close proximity to benefit each other by promoting their growth and creating a healthy environment for the plants to thrive.

Compost: A mixture of predominantly decaying organic matter used to fertilize the soil.

Container gardening: A garden grown in containers, such as pots or bags, instead of planting your crops in traditional in-ground gardens.

Cool-season crop: Often called winter-hardy plants, these are crops that thrive during colder temperatures. If you live in frosty climates, you should consider growing these types of plants.

Days to maturity: This is the number of days until a plant is able to produce flowers, fruits, and vegetables. You use this to determine when you should plant your seeds and when you can expect to harvest your first bounty.

Direct sowing: Planting seeds straight into the soil instead of growing your crops from seedlings.

Frost dates: This is the estimated date at which the air temperature drops so low that it can severely damage or kill your plants. It is often accompanied by frost.

Full sun: An area in your garden that gets about six hours of sun daily.

Germination: This is when your seeds start to grow into seedlings.

Growing: The physical increase in size over a period of time.

Growing or gardening zones: This refers to the best circumstances for gardening. It is determined by the climate of the region you live in.

Harvest: To pick, pluck, or collect vegetables and fruits from your garden.

Harvest category: The average length of time you can expect a specific plant to produce a harvest.

Mulch: This is a protective layer that you add to the top of your soil to maintain soil temperatures, control weeds, and decrease evaporation. This can be both organic and inorganic matter, including bark, pine needles, newspaper, and sawdust.

Organic matter: This refers to any type of material that used to be alive but is now in a varying state of decomposition. Adding organic matter to your garden can give your soil a fantastic boost.

Perennial plants: These are plants that can survive for three or more growing seasons.

Seed: Small grains or ovules of a plant with a hard casing. New plants grow from seeds after a process called germination.

Seedling: A young plant that hasn't reached maturity yet.

Soil ph: The measurement of the alkalinity or acidity of the soil.

Soil temperature: This is the measurement of the warmth of the soil. Ideally, the temperature of your soil should be between 65 and 75 °F (18 to 24 °C).

Succession planting: Staggering crops in terms of maturity dates will help you extend your harvest season, resulting in a continuous supply of produce straight from your garden.

Transplant: Repotting or moving a plant or seedling from one location or container to another.

Trellis: A structure, frame, or cage that can come in various patterns, shapes, or sizes used specifically for climbing or vining plants.

Warm-season crop: Plants that do well in both warm soil and air temperatures. It's best to plant these once the frost season is over.

CHAPTER 1: INTRODUCTION TO CONTAINER GARDENING

Imagine a life where you can enjoy home-grown vegetables every night for supper. You'll no longer have to spend hundreds of dollars every month to provide your family with the delicious and nutritious greens needed for healthy development and bodies. Unfortunately, not everyone has the extensive garden space to let their green fingers shine when growing their own crops. Luckily, all of this will change once you discover the wonderful world of container gardening.

With this gardening style, you can turn the smallest spaces into havens of greens and growth; believe it or not, a small corner of a balcony can be utilized to grow delicious freshness. Perhaps you have the garden space but don't want to create a traditional in-ground garden. It can be that an old back injury won't allow you to bend and kneel in a garden to take care of your crops. Even being wheelchair-bound no longer has to keep you from watching your vegetables grow from seeds (or seedlings, if you prefer).

So, if you're wondering what exactly container gardening entails, the amazing benefits it can bring to your life, or how to navigate some of the potential negatives that can come with this type of gardening, keep reading...

What Is Container Gardening?

Container gardens are exactly as the name suggests: a garden that is planted in containers rather than the traditional in-ground way of planting and growing crops where you plant your seeds or seedlings directly into the ground.

The containers used for container gardens can be anything from the more typical garden pots and crates to growing bags or any hollow-shaped bucket or bowl you might want to use. Even an old food bowl can be washed and used to grow vegetables. Reusing these old containers makes creating this type of garden friendly on your budget and the environment. In the next chapter, we'll discuss various tips to consider when choosing the ideal containers to use for your garden.

This type of garden is ideal for use when you have limited space, such as when you live in an apartment or house with a small garden or when you're renting a home where you either aren't allowed to change the garden landscape or don't want to spend the money to start a full vegetable garden that you can't take with you when you have to move. Even if you have the space for an in-ground garden, you may choose to use a container garden, as it's often easier to manage, as discussed in the coming chapters. For this reason, it's also ideal when you're just starting out with gardening and must still develop green fingers. Caring for a plant in a pot that you see constantly and have easy access to can be much easier than digging in the garden. Once you succeed at this type of gardening, you may gain the confidence needed to dig deeper into the gardening world and branch out, should you wish to do so.

Benefits of Container Gardening

While we've already touched on some of the amazing benefits you can gain by creating a container garden at your home, let's take this a step further to look at some of the most prominent advantages of growing your own crops in this way:

- You'll experience great flexibility in creating your garden. Apart from placing your containers in open areas around your home, you can also move them as the sun reaches those parts of your garden differently with the change in the seasons. You can move your containers indoors during cold months if you live in frosty areas or extreme climates.

- Depending on the size of your container, you'll typically need less soil to grow your crops than you would in a traditional garden. If you want to plant directly into the ground and the quality of your soil isn't good, buying enough top or potting soil for your garden can really do a number on your budget.

- If you want to grow crops with specific soil needs, altering the soil composition in container gardens is better than in-ground gardens. In Chapter 3, we'll discuss everything you need to know about soil selection and preparation.

- Since you won't use soil typically found in your area, you aren't limited to only growing crops native to your area or the soil type in your garden. You can easily experiment with other types of plants and companion plants, which we'll look at in Chapter 5.

- Your container garden can be a great addition to brightening dull areas around your home, particularly a paved or tiled area where you can't plant directly into the ground.

- You can place your container garden in busy areas of your home or yard where you frequently spend time. This will make it easier to care for your plants, as you don't have to go completely out of your way to weed or water your garden.

- Weeds are less likely to spread in container gardens than in traditional in-ground gardens, resulting in you having to spend much less time pulling weeds to keep your garden healthy and thriving.

- If you are disabled or wheelchair-bound, you can still create a garden using containers placed at a height that's comfortable for you to care for your plants. This isn't possible in an in-ground garden.

- Plants grown in containers are typically smaller than those planted in traditional in-ground gardens, as the size of the pot limits the development of their root systems. While serious gardeners may see this as a potential disadvantage, caring for a smaller plant is usually much easier than caring for a big one, which can make this type of gardening ideal for beginners. Harvesting your crops is also a much simpler task with container gardens than with in-ground alternatives, as we'll discuss in Chapter 10.

- If you go on vacation, you can take your smaller container plants either with you (unless you travel by airplane, of course) or to a friend to care for.

- The risk of pests in container gardens is significantly smaller than that of traditional in-ground gardens, resulting in healthier plants and easier pest control, as discussed in Chapter 7.

- Herbs usually thrive growing in pots, and if you place these containers close to your kitchen, you can easily grab some basil, thyme, or whatever else you might be growing while you're busy cooking.

Potential Negatives to Consider

As with any other project you might take on at home, there are some negatives to consider when you're starting a container garden. Being aware of these potential pitfalls will help you navigate them more effectively, as you'll be able to plan how to overcome these challenges to see your garden thrive. Let's look at some of the possible disadvantages you should consider when creating your garden:

- The soil in containers will dry quicker than in traditional in-ground gardens, as you can't rely on natural watering in the form of rain, and your plant's roots won't be able to grow deeper to reach wetter soil. As a result, you'll have to water your garden more frequently for your plants to gain the necessary nutrients to grow. In Chapter 9, we'll discuss everything you need to know about watering your container garden.

- Apart from possibly drying out quicker, your plants may also have a higher risk of suffering from nutrient deficiencies. This is because the soil can't replenish the nutrients absorbed by the plant from the surrounding soil, as would be the case in traditional in-ground gardens. Luckily, this potential pitfall can be managed using fertilizers and other nutrient management techniques, as discussed in Chapter 8.

- Not all vegetables can be grown successfully in containers. Some vegetables, such as carrots, need deeper soil than what you'll find in a typical container. If you decide to plant these, your crops will likely be smaller than you might want. In Chapter 5, we'll examine what plants typically thrive in containers.

- Unless you have garden equipment at home, you may have some initial start-up costs to get your garden going. However, there will be some costs involved in any type of garden you look to create, as you may also need some tools, soil, fertilizers, seeds, and seedlings, whether you create a traditional in-ground or container garden. In the next chapter, we'll provide you with a list of tools you might want to purchase to make your gardening experience easier.

As you can see, the many benefits of container gardening greatly outweigh any potential negatives that this might bring. Also, if you follow the strategies discussed in this book, these possible disadvantages can easily be managed. Still, starting a new project, such as a container garden, can be a daunting task, so to help you with this, we'll break it down into easy steps, starting in the next chapter with choosing the perfect container for your garden.

CHAPTER 2: CHOOSING THE RIGHT CONTAINERS

Choosing containers to use for your new garden can be a very exciting process. You might want to splurge on buying decorative ceramic pots that fit the decor of your home, grab a paintbrush and some paint to give old pots new life, or you might even decide to use old containers you have lying around as is to first test your gardening skills before you spend unnecessary money. Whatever you decide to do, you should remember that, just like not all containers are made the same, not all containers will yield the same crops. This doesn't mean you can't use any container to create a garden; it simply means you might have to take some additional steps to optimize your garden and crops.

I remember how unsure I was when I started my container garden. I had no idea what type of containers to use or what size these pots should be. I got some advice from my local gardening center, after which I researched the different plants I wanted to grow to better understand their needs (we'll discuss this in Chapter 5). I chose my containers according to what would work best for my plants and what I had available at home. I didn't want to spend hundreds of dollars on pots before I knew I could make my garden work. My container garden is an eclectic mix of plastic containers, ceramic pots, wooden barrels, and cloth bags for potatoes and carrots. I must admit, I absolutely love it!

To help you with this important step of choosing the right containers for your garden, we'll discuss everything you should consider, such as knowing what size container you should use, making sure your container has sufficient drainage, ensuring you take the necessary precautions according to the type of pot you use, and getting all the tools you'll need to care for your garden.

Size Does Matter

First, let's look at the size of the containers you choose to use. If you're completely new to gardening, you might opt for a bigger pot, as it can be easier to keep your plant healthy in these: They hold more soil, which means there will be more nutrients for the plants and more moisture in the soil. Smaller pots will dry out quicker, and, as a result, the plant will have to be watered more often. The same goes for small, hanging baskets where the soil will dry out quicker than in pots on the ground, particularly if you live in a windy area.

Always consider the soil and space needs of the plants you plan to grow. Average-sized vegetables require at least 12 inches of soil to thrive, although some larger vegetables may need significantly deeper soil (Sweetser, 2024c). For example, your tomatoes or squash plants with extensive root systems will do well in a five-gallon container, while shallow-rooted plants, like leafy greens, can do well in a smaller pot. The size of the container also directly impacts the size of the crops you grow. In smaller containers, the growth of your plants may be limited, resulting in smaller crops. In Chapter 5, we'll discuss the special needs of plants that typically do well in containers.

Another factor that is influenced by the pot's size is the soil's temperature. The temperature will be more constant in bigger pots, which means your plants' roots will be more protected from temperature changes, which is particularly important if you live in an area of severe climate change. Even the color of your container can play a role in how you care for your plants: the soil will stay cooler and moist for longer in light or cool-colored containers as opposed to dark or warm-colored ones, such as red, orange, or yellow.

If you plan to place your pots on a balcony, you'll have to consider the size of the pots and their weight once they are filled with moist soil. If your balcony isn't structurally strong, you may risk damaging the property if you use big, heavy pots. Smaller containers may be the best option if you're unsure of the weight your balcony can bear or if you must move your pots around to ensure they get enough sun throughout the year or to protect them against frost in the winter.

Consider the Drainage Holes

The next thing to consider when choosing containers for your garden is drainage holes. These holes at the bottom of the container are essential as they ensure your soil doesn't become waterlogged, which may result in your plants dying from root rot.

These holes typically don't have to be large. The container can either have one large hole in the middle or several smaller ones. If your container has a large hole at the bottom, your soil might drain through it. Testing the size of your drainage holes with the soil you plan to use before you create your garden can be helpful. If you find that the soil is draining at the bottom, you can place a coffee filter at the bottom of your container before adding the soil. This will keep the soil inside the pot while excess water drains.

Many decorative cachepots don't have drainage holes. The same will be the case if you choose to use an old bucket or food container for your garden. If your container doesn't have drainage holes, you can use a hand drill to create holes in them or place a smaller nursery pot with sufficient drainage holes inside the bigger pot. You can use the following rule of thumb should you have to add your own drainage holes (Sweetser, 2024c):

- Make sure your holes are around a quarter of an inch in size, as bigger holes will likely result in soil draining through them.

- You'll need between three and six holes if your pot is four to six inches in diameter. Bigger pots will need about six to eight drainage holes.

- If you live in a dry climate, you can opt for fewer holes as you'll want your soil to retain more moisture, but if you live in humid environments, you can add an extra hole or two to ensure more airflow and drainage.

Different Types of Containers

Now that you have a better idea of the size and drainage requirements of your container, let's turn our focus to what it's made of. When you go to your local nursery store, you may be surprised at the many options for different available materials. Each of these options comes with its own advantages and disadvantages. Making an informed decision on what you want will require you to understand the pros and cons of each type of material and consider what will work for the garden you hope to create.

Plastic

These containers are popular options as they are usually reasonably inexpensive, come in a wide variety of colors, shapes, and sizes, and are lightweight, so you can easily move the containers around even when they are filled with soil. Unfortunately, the plastic can become brittle if the containers stand in the sun or are exposed to extremely cold weather. For this reason, it's best to choose plastic containers that are both sturdy and somewhat flexible. Also, if you're growing vegetables, make sure the containers are made from food-grade plastic to avoid harmful chemicals leaching into the soil.

Terracotta or Clay

Terracotta or clay pots are often very attractive and decorative options to use for creating a garden, especially if this garden will be placed in an area you will often be in or where you might entertain guests. Unfortunately, these pots can break easily or get damaged by frost. If you live in a cold climate, you must bring these pots inside during the colder months. As a result, these pots aren't suitable for hardy plants that will remain outside year-round.

You'll also have to pay close attention to the quality of your soil when using terracotta or clay pots, as the moisture in the soil will be absorbed by the pot, resulting in the soil drying quickly. Due to this, you'll have to water your plant more frequently. Alternatively, you can line the pot with a smaller, plastic nursery pot or use a paintbrush to add a layer of transparent lead-free glaze.

Once filled with soil, these containers will be significantly heavier than plastic ones, which is something to consider if you must move your pots around during extreme weather conditions. Again, if you use a plastic pot inside the terracotta or clay pot, you can remove the plastic pot when you need to move the container.

Concrete

Cast concrete can be an excellent option if you plan to never move your garden. These containers come in various sizes and styles and you can even use old cinder blocks to plant your crops in. The great benefit of this type of container is that you can keep them outside year-round regardless of the climate you stay in; these containers won't get damaged in extreme weather conditions.

However, as you can imagine, these containers will be extremely heavy, especially when filled with soil. As a result, they aren't always suitable for use on decks or balconies. Concrete and fiberglass blends are much lighter alternatives if you still want the concrete look.

Polyurethane Foam

Containers made from polyurethane foam are fantastic options if you like the look of terracotta, clay, or concrete containers but want a lighter pot that you can move. These containers also won't chip or crack as easily as the real deal, and since they provide excellent insulation for the soil and the plant's roots, they are good options if you live in an area with severe weather conditions. You can leave these containers outside year-round.

Wood

Wooden containers are possibly the most natural-looking of all the options available. The wood serves as a great insulator, protecting the soil and roots of the plant from big temperature changes. Another massive pro of this type of container is that you can make your own planter boxes in the exact size and shape you require. If you do build your own boxes, it's best to use rot-resistant wood, such as cedar or locust. You can also use a cheaper alternative, such as pine, if you treat the wood before you plant it. If rot does set into your planter box, you'll have to replace it to avoid spoiling your plants and crops.

Grow Bags

Grow bags are essentially "pots" made from fabric. They are lightweight and breathable, allowing enough airflow to your plant's roots. They often come with handles, making moving them around easier. Moreover, these bags can easily be washed for reuse should you use them for seasonal plants.

A con about using these bags is that, water will drain from the soil quickly since they are highly breathable. As a result, you'll likely have to water your plants more frequently to prevent the soil from drying out.

Metal

While many people choose to use metal containers for their gardens due to their durability, these won't be a good option if you live in extreme weather conditions. Metal conducts heat and will expose your soil and roots to rapid fluctuations in temperature.

Recycled Containers

Big plastic buckets or old toy bins that you might have around the house can also be used as inexpensive plant boxes. Just ensure you add drainage holes to them before you add your soil.

Tools You'll Need

Once you've decided on what container you want to use and checked that it has sufficient drainage holes, you're almost ready to start adding soil and planting your seeds or seedlings. However, before you do this, it can be helpful to ensure you have all the tools you might need for your garden. While you don't have to buy every gardening gadget that your local nursery stocks, there are a few essentials you should consider getting to make this process easier for you and give your plants the best chance of thriving.

Hand Trowel

This important tool is almost like a mini garden spade and is usually the first piece of equipment you'll buy when you start with your garden. It's an extremely useful tool and can be used for mixing soil, digging in the soil, planting seedlings, leveling the soil, and scooping and adding compost, fertilizer, or potting mix.

When you look at buying a hand trowel, you'll see various options, including ones made from different types of metal and plastic. I would suggest you look for one made from heavy metal, such as steel, iron, or carbon steel, as these trowels are strong and won't bend easily when working the soil. While these trowels will be more expensive than those made from plastic or aluminum, the heavy metal ones will last you much longer than the cheaper alternatives, making them a good investment. Some of these trowels also have inch markings on the side, making measuring exactly how deep you're digging easy.

Also, since you'll be working with your hand trowel quite a bit, ensure the handle has a comfortable yet sturdy grip, ideally with a rubber coating. Many of these have a loop at the end of the handle, making it easy to hang your tool up neatly after you've used it.

Hand Cultivator

This tool is similar to a hand trowel, only instead of a spade in the front, it has three or more prongs that make tilling your soil, removing weeds, and mixing fertilizers into the soil easier. Again, make sure your cultivator is made from hard metal that won't bend easily and that it has a comfortable grip on the handle.

Pruner

This is often called a garden shear, like a strong scissor used to cut stems and even small branches. It can even be used to harvest some of your crops. When buying a pruner, make sure that the blades are sharp, don't need frequent sharpening, and are made from rust-proof material. Also, ensure your blades have a locking mechanism, as this will help prevent accidental injuries.

Gardening Gloves

Gardening gloves aren't just vital to prevent your hands from becoming muddy; they also protect your hands from thorns and insect bites or stings. If you have sensitive skin, gloves can help prevent skin irritations, particularly if you might be allergic to some of the fluids often found in the branches and stems of plants. Long-sleeve garden gloves can be a great buy if you have sensitive skin, and if you're working with thorny plants, opt for thornproof ones.

Watering Can

Using a garden hose is often impossible when caring for a container garden. Unless you constantly want to walk up and down with a jug, using a watering jug can be vital, especially if you choose one with a long spout to help you reach the pots you might have behind other plants. Also, make sure you choose a watering can that won't be too heavy to carry and handle when it's filled. If your plants are all within easy reach or you fear overwatering your crops, you can use a watering can with a showerhead attachment on the spout.

Kneeling Pad

Whether you opt for a traditional in-ground or container garden, you'll spend much time kneeling next to your plants to weed, prune, and harvest your crops. This can do a number on your knees, particularly if your containers stand on a hard surface. A kneeling pad can help save your knees while kneeling. Just make sure you choose one with a waterproof cover so that the sponge inside the pad won't spoil if it gets wet, which is bound to happen. If you don't want to spend money on a kneeling pad, you can also use an old pillow that you don't mind getting damaged.

Soil Scoop

This scoop is similar to the ones you might use to scoop pet food and is very handy when you have to scoop fertilizer or compost into your garden. Always make sure you choose a scoop with high-side walls, as this will make it easier to scoop larger volumes at a time. It's also good to look for a material that won't rust, such as good steel or plastic.

Micro-Tip Scissors

These are tiny scissors with long, pointed blades that are ideal to use when caring for seedlings or delicate, smaller plants, as you'll be able to prune and harvest with much more precision and care. Again, make sure you opt to buy scissors made from rust-proof material with a locking mechanism to prevent accidental injuries.

Plant Supports

When creating a garden in a limited space, you might want to take advantage of as much vertical space as possible. Many plants do excellent when grown in support cages or over stakes, such as tomatoes, peppers, and beans. You can choose from many supports, such as cages, bamboo or steel stakes, or vining trellis. Regardless of what you decide to use, make sure it's sturdy and won't rust or potentially spoil your crops. Also, ensure you get the necessary ties or twines to support your plant properly.

Plant Labels

When you plant your seeds or seedlings, you might know exactly where you're placing them. Once these plants start harvesting crops, there will be obvious signs in the fruits and vegetables. But, before that happens, you might have difficulty remembering which is which. This is where plant labels come in handy, particularly if you add the date on which the plant is placed in the ground to the label. Always make sure you use waterproof labels and fade-proof ink. Painting the names on river rocks can also be an excellent option to label your plants.

Soil Moisture Meter

If you're new to gardening or unsure how to maintain your soil's moisture. A moisture meter can be a fantastic addition to your gardening toolbox. This device keeps track of the moisture in your soil, making it easy to know when you need to water your plants and when you've overwatered your garden.

Self-Watering Spikes

If you fear that you might forget to water your plants, using self-watering spikes can save your garden. This device turns any water bottle you might have around your home into a slow-releasing drip system. Simply add the spike to a filled water bottle, turn it upside down, and insert it into the soil close to the plant. Now, you only have to make sure there is water in the bottle.

Plant Dolly

If you like the look of heavy containers but don't have the strength to move them in case of severe weather or to make sure your plants get sufficient sunlight throughout the year, a plant dolly might be the answer you've been looking for. This is basically a platform that stands on wheels that you place your container onto.

Caring For Your Gardening Tools

Since you'll likely have quite a few different tools to care for and maintain your garden, it can be helpful to get a tool bag or tool caddy to store all your tools. When you go out to your garden, you can simply grab your tool bag or caddy and know that you'll have everything you might need with you, avoiding having to walk up and down to get something. I always add a few plastic bags to my caddy to immediately discard waste materials.

After you've used your tools, it's important that you take the necessary steps to care for them. This will not only boost the durability and longevity of your tools but also protect your plants from any diseases that might end up on your tools. These are the steps I take with my gardening tools:

- Rinse your tools with water and dry them with a rag or paper towel. Make sure the tools are completely dry before you pack them away.
- Do a deep cleaning of your gardening tools once a month by either wiping them with hand sanitizer or placing them in bleach for a few minutes.
- Clean all your plant supports after the harvesting season has ended.
- Wipe your pruners or scissor blades with WD-40 or similar gardening oil to lubricate them. Non-stick kitchen spray can work just as well.
- Make sure you store your gardening tools indoors to prevent rust or bending in adverse weather conditions.

While these are the gardening tools I simply can't be without, your list of must-have tools might look completely different. Since this largely depends on your personal preference, feel free to add your favorites to your tool bag or caddy.

Once you've selected your container, made sure it has sufficient drainage holes, and compiled your gardening toolbox, it's time to get the soil ready to start your garden. In the next chapter, we'll examine everything you need to know about soil selection and preparation.

CHAPTER 3: SOIL SELECTION AND PREPARATION

Soil is so much more than brown sand, which houses your plant's root system. Never let the color of the soil confuse you; experienced gardeners will quickly tell you that soil should be regarded as the gold that can make or break your garden. Soil that is rich in minerals and nutrients will be like an all-you-can-eat buffet for your plants, where they can absorb exactly what they need when they need it.

Unfortunately, even some proficient gardeners may have trouble knowing what soil will be best for your plants and how to alter your soil to create a proper breakfast buffet for your plants. I've also been there, believing I can just scoop some soil from my existing garden to my container garden. As a newbie gardener, I couldn't understand why my plants didn't thrive or why my neighbor's garden was filled with strawberries while mine barely made any buds. After extensive research and speaking to the experts at my local nursery, my problem became clear: I didn't select the right soil. I gave up on my existing plants and started all over from scratch, this time making sure I used the perfect blend of organic soil. You might already guess what happened. Within a few weeks, I had the most beautiful strawberry plants filled with many bright red fruits.

To help you avoid making the same mistakes I made when I started, we'll now discuss the importance of selecting good soil for your garden, how to amend your soil for optimal plant growth, and tried and tested tips on how to best fill your containers.

Importance of Using the Right Soil

Healthy plants need to grow in healthy soil filled with nutrients. Unfortunately, the soil you typically find in your garden, regardless of where you live, won't offer your crops the natural goodness they need. Depending on where you stay, your garden soil may be heavy and dense, become easily waterlogged and compacted, resulting in a lack of airflow to your plant's roots, and often carry disease or insects. Conversely, your garden soil might even be sandy with the water draining through it too quickly and easily.

Instead, potting soil mixes are typically ideal, especially those specifically designed for use in containers. A good potting soil mix will drain quickly without leaving your soil dry, is lightweight, and should be free from any pests, including disease, insects, and weeds. It's also aerated, which means airflow can easily move through the soil to reach the plant's roots.

The magic about potting soil is that, it doesn't contain any actual soil, despite what the name suggests. It combines many different organic ingredients, such as vermiculite, coconut husks, sphagnum peat moss, and bark. Some even contain additives such as ground limestone and granulated fertilizers, reducing your need to add additional fertilizer, at least for the first few months. All of these components provide your plants with the perfect blend of nutrients and texture for your plants to develop strong and sturdy root systems.

Now, when you go to your local nursery store, you might see bags of topsoil. Even though it contains the word "soil," it doesn't contain the special components that your plants need for healthy growth. These bags of topsoil are usually used to fill up low spots in your garden or to level your lawn, not for growing fruits and vegetables. If you want to use topsoil for your container garden, you'll have to add some of the vital nutrients yourself, as discussed below.

Choosing the Right Soils

Now that you know to opt for potting soil, you might still be confused by the wide variety of different options that your local nursery might stock. You can use the following checklist to make sure you choose potting soil that has the right blend of nutrients as well as the perfect texture and moisture retention for the garden you plan to grow:

- **Check the labels:** Always read the label on the potting soil to ensure it wasn't created for a specific type of plant. You'll often find that some soils were made for delicate flowers, such as orchids, while others were designed for certain types of vegetables only. If you want to grow various crops, it's best to use general planting soil for containers.

- **Look at the ingredient list:** Read through the ingredients in the potting soil to ensure you choose one with an average amount of each component. You don't want to use potting soil with too much sand or bark in it, as this can impact the development of your plant's root systems.

- **Feel the consistency:** This step isn't always possible, as some nurseries either won't have open bags of potting soil or won't be willing to open one for you. But, if you can, check the consistency to ensure it's fluffy for good drainage and that there aren't too many big pieces of bark in the mixture. You can also smell the soil; a good potting soil will have a pleasant scent. Other things to look out for include:

  - Make sure there are no insects in the soil.

  - Ensure it's not sandy or overly coarse.

  - Feel that the potting mix is moist but not soggy.

  - See if clumps of soil will break apart when touched. This will ensure the soil is porous so that water and air can reach your plants' roots.

  - Avoid buying any potting soil that smells rotten or stinky.

- **Consider your container:** Look at the weight of the soil. No, I'm not talking about the size of the bag but rather how heavy a handful feels when you're holding it. Some potting soils are heavier than others and might be too heavy to use in hanging baskets or weighty containers on balconies. Always remember that once you add water to your soil, it will be even heavier and add to your container's overall weight. Potting soil with a high compost composition is typically heavier, while a soilless mixture rich in coco coir and peat moss is ideal for use in hanging baskets.

Soil Amendments for Container Gardening

If you choose to use topsoil for your garden and want to alter it yourself to optimize the nutritional value of your plants, there are many ingredients you can add. It is, however, important that you understand the role each of these ingredients plays in the composition of your soil. Some of the most commonly used ones include:

- **Biochar:** A porous carbon-rich compound that aids the aeration and drainage of your soil, helps with nutrient and moisture retention, maintains soil pH, and boosts soil biodiversity.

- **Compost:** This magical goodness enhances nutrient levels, soil structure, drainage, moisture retention, and microbe biodiversity. We'll discuss compost in more detail in the next chapter.

- **Mycorrhizal fungi:** You might not think that adding fungi can be good for your soil, but mycorrhizal fungi help increase water and nutrients around the plant's roots.

- **Perlite:** This lightweight volcanic rock is added to improve drainage and aeration. It's generally considered to be a good replacement for sand in your soil mixture, which can be ideal if you want to keep your soil as light as possible.

- **Vermiculite:** This mineral prevents nutrients from leaching away, retains moisture, decreases density, and improves the plant's uptake of potassium and magnesium. If you add vermiculite to your soil, make sure that you handle it gently, as it can easily compact and lose its air-holding ability if overhandled.

- **Coarse sand:** Builder's or coarse sand can be used to improve aeration as it loosens the soil. If your plant is top-heavy, adding coarse sand to your soil will add weight to the container, which can help prevent it from tipping over.

- **Sphagnum peat moss:** This decomposed form of moss clings to the water and provides nutrients to stop it from washing away. However, peat moss compacts over time, which can lead to water retention and root suffocation. If you choose to add sphagnum peat moss to your soil, you'll have to ensure that the soil is loosened properly before you plant your seeds or seedlings and use it for seasonal plants only.

- **Pine bark:** This potting mix ingredient is fantastic for adding aeration to your soil but has poor water-holding abilities. However, since it degrades slowly, adding longevity to your soil mixture is a good option. It can be used as a replacement for peat moss.

- **Coir:** This tubular fiber is a byproduct of coconuts and contains no twigs or sticks. It typically comes as a compressed brick that expands and breaks apart when adding water. They are great to use as a nitrogen supplement, but since salt water is usually used to create the bricks, it can result in salt damage to your plants. Washing the coir with clean water before you add it to your soil mixture can minimize this risk.

- **Dolomitic limestone:** This form of limestone is great for adding magnesium to your soil, which is a very important nutrient for your plants. It's also vital if the pH level of your soil is off, as this can help to neutralize soil acidity.

Always remember that when you add to your soil mixture, it's always best to keep your soil as lightweight as possible (unless you purposefully want heavier soil). This will help your plant's root systems develop, transport more water to the roots, improve airflow to the plant, and boost drainage to prevent your soil from becoming waterlogged.

Creating a Balanced Potting Mix

While the information above will help you understand how the various ingredients can impact your soil, you may still feel unsure of how much of each one you want to add if you're ever creating your own potting mix. I remember the first time I made my own potting soil. I went to my local nursery with a list of ingredients that I wanted to add to my soil. But, when I got home, my confidence took an absolute nose-dive, as I just didn't know what combinations and quantities to use. After doing extensive research, I found these recipes to be valuable in getting the ratios perfect.

Basic Container Potting Mix

This is probably one of the easiest recipes to make and can be used to grow pretty much any plants that typically do well in containers. This recipe makes enough potting soil to fill around two 14-inch containers. I measured the ingredients using a four-gallon bucket (around one liter). To make this potting soil, simply mix these ingredients:

- 1 bucket coir
- 1/2 bucket compost
- 1/2 bucket vermiculite
- 1/2 bucket perlite
- 2 cups time-release fertilizer (we'll discuss this in more detail in Chapter 8)
- 2 cups coarse sand

Garden Soil Potting Mix

This recipe is perfect if you want to use your garden soil as the base for your potting soil. By altering the composition of the soil, you'll add the nutrients your plant will need and adjust the pH levels sufficiently for your garden to thrive. To make this soil, mix the following ingredients together and add sufficient amount of water to ensure it's not dry:

- 2 gallons of garden soil
- 2 gallons of compost of your choice
- 2 gallons perlite
- 2 gallons of peat moss
- 1/2 cup kelp powder
- 1/2 cup dolomitic limestone
- 1/2 cup greensand
- 1/2 cup rock phosphate
- 1/2 cup soybean meal

Homemade Soilless Mix

When I first started gardening, I struggled to wrap my head around the idea of a soilless potting mix. I bought bags full at my local nursery, but had to build up a lot of confidence before I decided to create my own soilless mixes. However, once I made my first one, I was surprised at how easy it actually was. The key to this is to moisten it well with water during the mixing process, as it can be hard to wet initially.

- 8 gallons of peat moss
- 8 gallons vermiculite or perlite

- 1/2 pound dolomitic limestone
- 1 1/2 ounces of phosphate fertilizer
- 1 pound fertilizer

Filling Your Pots

Now that you have your potting soil ready (either homemade or store-bought), let's focus on filling your containers. Yes, you might think that you can simply throw your soil into your containers and be done with it. While this can be true, it's always best to follow the proper steps to give your garden the best chance to thrive:

- **Clean your containers:** Whether using brand-new pots or repurposing containers you might have around the home, you should always ensure you clean them properly. There might be harmful bacteria lurking in your containers, which can affect the health of your soil and plants. To clean your containers, you can simply create a diluted bleach solution to wash them. Make sure you dry your containers properly before you add your soil.

- **Check your drainage holes:** Next, you can compare the size of the drainage holes with the soil you plan to use. You're good to go if your drainage holes are small enough that your soil won't filter through them. However, if your holes are big and you're using fine soil, you can add coffee filters, a layer of newspaper or paper towels, or pebbles to the bottom of your container. Remember that pebbles will add to the weight of your container and reduce the amount of soil in your pot, so only use them if you use a big container or don't plan to move your filled pot.

- **Place your containers:** Before you add your soil, it's best to place your containers where you want to grow your garden. Once your containers are filled, they may be too heavy for you to move around. After placing your containers, I would suggest you wait a few days to keep an eye on how much sun your plants will get. The amount of sunlight your plants need will depend on the type of vegetables you want to grow, as we'll discuss in Chapter 5. Also, consider your plant's watering needs and how much water your soil will lose if they have sun all day. If keeping them watered during the day is a problem, look for sites that receive morning sun but get shade during the hottest part of the day, even if you're growing plants for full sun. Afternoon shade will reduce the amount of moisture your plants need.

- **Add your soil:** Once you've removed the drainage holes in your container, you can add your soil. Consider the plants you hope to grow in the container to ensure you add enough soil for the plant's roots to develop.

- **Water your soil:** This is a very important step that many newbie gardeners skip. Once you've added your soil to your container, you should moisten your soil by flooding your containers a few times and stirring properly to ensure the soil is loosened and thoroughly moistened.

- **Add your plants:** Once your soil is ready and thoroughly moistened (but not waterlogged), you can add or plant your seedlings. Loosen the soil by creating a hole big enough for the existing root system of your seedling. Remove your seedlings from the container they came in and take as much care as possible to not disrupt their root systems. Place it into the soil and close any gaps around the plant's roots with the soil. Always plant your seedlings at the same depth as they were in the container you bought them in. If you want to grow from seeds, follow the instructions on the packet. We'll discuss the difference between seeds and seedlings in Chapter 6.

- **Water your plants:** After you've planted your seedlings or seeds, you should water your soil again. ensure you don't flush the seeds open or damage your delicate seedlings while watering.

Just when you think you understand the soil your garden needs to thrive, it's time to turn our attention to another important factor all avid gardeners should understand: composting your garden. In the next chapter, we'll look at the many benefits your garden can gain from proper composting, how you can easily create your own compost at home, and specific things to look out for when buying compost at your local nursery.

CHAPTER 4: COMPOSTING ON A SMALL SCALE

When preparing food in the kitchen, do you throw your vegetable peels and other scraps in the dustbin? What about fruits that you left in the fridge way too long and have since become rotten? Or your eggshells, coffee paper filters, or old tea bags? What if I tell you that instead of binning these items, you can use them to boost your soil and nourish your plants?

This is where the magic of composting comes in. In short, it's a wonderful way to recycle waste from your kitchen and yard to feed your garden. As a result, if you're growing fruit and vegetables, your waste will literally feed you again. While you can buy bags of specially created compost at your local nursery, you can easily make your own at home. The good news is that you don't need to have a massive garden to do this. If you want to take this a step further, you can even create your own worm farm for vermicomposting. It is much easier than you might think.

To help you turn your trash into gardening gold, we'll now discuss everything you need to know about composting, including the benefits, how to create your own compost despite perhaps not having extensive space, and how to avoid making common mistakes.

What Is Composting?

Before we discuss how to create your own compost and what you should and shouldn't add to your compost bin or heap, let's discuss what exactly composting entails. With the risk of oversimplifying this, composting is when organic matter, such as leaves and food scraps, breaks down into the soil. This happens when these products decompose in a process created by fungi, bacteria, and insects such as worms and sow bugs. The final product from this decomposition, which looks similar to garden soil, is called compost.

Since compost is rich in nutrients and benefits your garden and plants, it's often referred to in gardening circles as "black gold." This is because, through this process of decomposition and interaction with organisms, the dark, rich compost gets filled with many different beneficial microbes. This enriches the soil by adding nutrients and improving the retention of water. If your soil becomes compacted or hard, adding compost can even help to break up the soil, improving aeration and giving your plant's roots space to develop. The microbes will also help to reduce pests and diseases in your soil and plants.

When you add compost regularly to your garden, you reduce the need for chemical fertilizers. This is very important if you want to grow vegetables, as many synthetic fertilizers contain chemicals that can harm your plants and affect your crops. We'll have a deeper look at fertilizers, when to use them, and how to choose the best ones for a vegetable garden in Chapter 8.

By creating your own compost, you're also doing your bit for the environment, as your kitchen and garden scraps won't end up in landfills where they will emit greenhouse gases like methane.

How Composting Works

Now that you have a better understanding of what composting is, let's turn our focus to how this process actually works and what is meant when experienced gardeners refer to layering greens and browns in their compost bins. While decomposition will happen naturally when you leave these items out to rot, adding the right mixture of these two ingredients with sufficient airflow and water can accelerate this decomposition.

When you add a good mixture of both of these ingredients, combined with air and water, you can accelerate this decomposition process. This will give the organisms in your compost bins the ideal living conditions to work through the matter you add to the bin. Let's look at all the aspects needed for quick production of composts:

- **Greens**: These are the nitrogen additions to your compost bin and are vitally important for the growth and reproduction of plants and other organic matter, which will result in rich compost to mix in your potting soil. There are many different household waste products you can add to your compost bin to make up the greens, including food scraps, coffee grounds, and fresh grass clippings. If your compost bin ever gets slimy, stinky, and wet, it's usually a sign that you've added too many greens. You can rectify this by adding more browns.

- **Browns**: These are the carbon additions to your compost bins and provide food for the organisms living in your bin. Common examples of good browns to add to your compost bin include branches, dead leaves, twigs, and paper. If you find that your compost bin is dry and doesn't produce compost fast enough, it's usually a sign that you've added too much brown. The ideal ratio to aim for is adding between two and four parts brown for every part green you have.

- **Airflow**: Just like any other living organism, the decomposers in your compost bin need air to survive. You can boost the airflow in your bin by ensuring everything you add is finely broken or chopped up and turning the piles often. I have a long stick next to my bin to stir the contents once a week during the summer and every few weeks during the colder months. Proper airflow in your bin will also reduce smells. You can also drill holes into your compost bin or even just stick a PVC pipe in it to increase airflow.

- **Water**: The decomposers in your bin will also need water to thrive and produce compost. The perfect mixture of moisture in your compost bin should resemble that of a damp sponge; if you take a handful of your mixture and squeeze it, it should be wet to the touch, but no water should drip out. In many cases, the greens you add to your compost bin will provide sufficient moisture for your organisms. However, if you find that your compost bin runs dry, you can sprinkle some water into it.

- **Temperature**: If at all possible, try to raise the temperature in your compost bin, as this will aid the growth of aerobic organisms and produce compost more quickly. The ideal temperature for aerobic composting is between 130 and 140° Fahrenheit. If you don't want to invest in special lights to raise the temperature, you can simply make sure you place your compost bin in a hot, sunny area in your garden, and if you use a bin instead of a pile, you can use a dark-colored bin.

Waste to Add to Your Compost

I remember when I started my first compost bin, and I was pleasantly surprised at how many waste products I could repurpose in this way for my garden rather than to fill my dustbin. I got to a point where I would grab my phone every time I had to throw something away check if it couldn't be composted. To save you the time of repeatedly searching for these answers online, I've created a list of household waste you can toss in your compost bin:

- Rotten fruit and vegetables
- Peels and scraps from fruit and vegetables
- Trimmings from houseplants
- Tea leaves and tea bags
- Coffee grounds and filters
- Eggshells
- Napkins, unused toilet paper, and paper towels
- Shredded paper, cardboard, and newspaper
- Hair and fur
- Leaves
- Grass clippings

- Yard trimmings
- Flowers
- Sawdust

Waste That Should Never End Up in Your Compost Bin

Not all kitchen and garden waste should end up in your compost bin. Some of these items could contain harmful toxins, attract rodents and unwanted insects, and give your bin a foul odor. Items that should never be composted include:

- Scraps and bones from poultry, meat, and fish.
- Dairy products
- Any part of a walnut, including the leaves and twigs from a walnut tree, releases compounds that can be toxic to other plants.
- Large pieces of wood
- Charcoal and ash
- Grease, cooking oil, and fat
- Any yard trimmings that have been treated with pesticides
- Baked food scraps
- Plants with diseases or covered in insects
- Pet waste

- Coffee pods

How to Make Your Own Compost

There are many ways in which you can compost. It's best that you choose the method best suited to your individual needs and circumstances. This can include using a composting bin, a compost tumbler, or a designated compost pile if you have enough yard space. If you go for creating a pile, you should have an open space of at least three feet that you can allocate for creating your black gold. If you're going for contained composting (so not doing it in a loose pile), you can use almost any bin you might have at home. However, if you're new to this, I would suggest you get a special composting bin. These bins have an opening at the bottom through which you can easily remove the black gold that is ready for use in your garden.

Compost tumblers are also excellent for creating your own compost. As the name suggests, these bins usually hang on a stand, making it very easy to turn and mix your compost to yield optimal results. They can close completely, reducing the risk of odors, rodents, and other pests entering it and affecting the quality of your compost. These tumblers typically don't take up a lot of space, making them ideal if you live in an apartment or don't have extensive yard space. Once you've decided whether you want to use a bin, tumbler, or the traditional pile, you can follow these steps:

- **Decide on a location:** Choosing the ideal location isn't as simple as just placing your bin in an open space in your yard. It should ideally be in a place that gets equal amounts of sun and shade and has good drainage. If you live in a climate that gets lots of rain, consider choosing an undercover location to limit the amount of water in your compost bin. Alternatively, if you live in a very hot climate, you should create your compost in a shady place to avoid drying your bin. You should also consider your ease of access to the pile or bin. If it's a big schlep to add your waste, you might not stick to the process and throw your food scraps in the dust bin instead of composting your garden.

- **Add your compostable materials:** Once you've decided on a location and placed your bin or tumbler (if you choose one of these), you can start to add your compostable materials. If possible, it's best to create layers of your greens and browns, as this will help to speed up the decomposition of your matter to create your compost. I believe it's best to start with a layer of bulky browns, as this will aid aeration and drainage in your bin. If you see that the compostable materials are very dry, you can sprinkle some water in between every layer. Always remember to shred your materials as finely as possible to speed up decomposition.

- **Turn your pile regularly:** After adding your compostable materials, you can leave it for a week or so to rest. Then, you should start to turn your pile to improve aeration and disperse moisture. This is easy to do if you use a tumbler. If you opt for a bin or a pile, you can use a stick, a shovel, or a pitchfork to rotate the materials.

- **Start using your compost:** Depending on the care you take in maintaining your compost bin as well as important factors such as aeration, moisture, the ratio of greens and browns, and temperature, it can take anything from a few weeks to a year to yield your first compost. When it's ready to use, your compost will look like dark soil.

Once you've filled your compost bin or pile, you shouldn't continue to add fresh material. If you do, you will slow down the decomposition of your materials so that your compost may never be ready for use. Ideally, you also don't want to wait for the weeks to months it might take for your compost to be ready before you start working on your next batch. For this reason, I highly recommend that you create more than one bin or pile at a time. This way, you'll continuously be able to repurpose your scraps to create black gold as well as have a constant supply of compost for your garden. I always have three bins going: one ready for use, one busy decomposing, and one where I add waste products.

When your compost seems ready, you might find some material hasn't properly decomposed yet. This is usually material like corn cobs or eggshells that can take longer than, for example, potato peels. You can simply remove the undecomposed material from your ready-to-use compost and add it to the batch that's still in progress. It can also happen that the top layer of your pile decomposes slower than the rest. You can simply remove this layer and add it to your in-progress bin.

Another way to speed up the process of producing compost is by adding a scoop or two of your ready-made compost or store-bought compost to your new batch. This compost will contain all the decomposers you want working in your bin, boosting the population of organisms doing the hard work.

Consider Vermicomposting at home

If you're feeling adventurous about creating your own compost, or once you've gotten the hang of a more traditional compost bin or pile, you can try your hand at creating your own vermicompost at home. In short, this process uses earthworms to aid in the decomposition of your materials, providing nutrient-rich compost for your garden. In the case of vermicomposting, the worms will excrete the compost. Doing this doesn't mean you can scratch in your existing garden to collect earthworms. These soil-dwelling worms won't process large amounts of food waste and typically don't do well in confined spaces. Instead, redworms, or red wigglers, as they are commonly known, are ideal, as they not only produce rapidly but also prefer to stay in a specific area. Most nurseries and pet shops stock these worms, or you can even order them online.

Creating a worm farm, as vermicomposting is often referred to, is much easier than many people will think. You can use any type of container or even build your own worm bin from wood. Alternatively, you can purchase commercial bins specifically created for worm farms. I used two plastic containers for my worm farm that fit into each other. I drilled several holes in them to ensure proper airflow to my compost. I also drilled holes in the bottom of the top container (which slides into the other one). This way, the black gold could drain into the bottom container once it's ready, and I don't have to handle the worms too often to try to remove the ready-to-use compost (the worm poop). I also drilled holes in the lid of the top container.

Once your bins are ready, you can fill about half the bin with moist, shredded newspaper or paper towels. You can also add a handful or two of plain garden soil, as this will add some microorganisms that will aid your worms in doing their job. Next, you can add your worms and place your bin in a dark and cool, location with few temperature fluctuations. I placed mine in the basement, but a dark cupboard, your shed, or a garage can work just as well.

You can feed your worms the same food scraps and household waste you would add to a traditional compost bin. If you see that your worm farm is getting dark, you can add water gently using a spray bottle. To help my worms digest the food as quickly as possible, I always make sure I shred the food scraps finely. I also took care to place this "food" in a different location at the top of the bin so that I could keep track of how much my worms were eating. This helped me time their next feed and portions better. Remember, as your worm population grows (and it happens rather quickly), you'll have to increase the amount of food scrap you provide them.

When you add food or moisture, try to do this as quickly as possible, as these worms work best when they aren't disturbed. For example, every time you open the lid to add food, they will instantly stop feeding and search for cover under the soil or newspaper. Once you're ready to harvest your compost, you can simply lift the top container out of the bottom one and scoop your vermicompost out. Alternatively, you can also dump the entire contents of your worm farm onto a tarp and separate the finished material from the undecomposed ones. Then, you can replace the shredded newspaper and add your worms back into the container to start fresh.

Adding Compost to Your Container

If you're wondering what to do with your compost after its creation, this next section is for you. While there are many different ways of adding compost to your container garden, I found the next three methods to work easiest:

- **Mixing with potting soil:** If you aren't sure of the quality of the potting soil you're using or if you simply want to optimize the soil for your plants, you can blend compost with potting soil before you plant your seedlings or seeds. The ideal ratio to use should be around one part compost to about three parts potting soil. This will help create a good balance of nutrients while also providing good drainage.

- **Top dressing or mulching:** If your garden is already in process, you can sprinkle a layer of compost on top of the soil. This will serve the same purpose as mulch typically does and help your soil retain moisture while adding nutrients and encouraging beneficial microbial activity. It can also suppress the growth of weeds if used as mulch and protect your soil from temperature fluctuations.

- **Compost tea:** This is basically a nutrient-rich liquid fertilizer made from your compost and can give your plants an excellent boost in growth. Making this tea is surprisingly easy. Simply mix your compost with water and let it rest for about a day or two. Then, strain this mixture, pour it into a spray bottle, and spray it directly onto your plant.

As much as compost is highly beneficial for your plants, it should always be used in moderation. Adding too much compost to your potting soil, can negatively affect the soil's drainage. The soil can even become too nutrient-rich for some of the plants you might be growing. I always take the less-is-more approach, where I'll add a little to moderate amount of compost to my soil and then see how my plants respond over a period of two to three weeks. You can easily add more compost should your plants need it, but reducing the amount of compost is much more difficult as you'll have to add more soil and ensure you mix the new soil well with your existing soil, all without disturbing your plant's roots.

Now that your soil is ready and your compost bin is well on its way to producing black gold for your plants to thrive, let's go over to arguably the most exciting part of gardening: choosing which plants you want to grow. In the next chapter, we'll discuss different fruits and vegetables that typically do well when grown in containers, as well as seasonal planting for different climates and the importance of companion plants.

CHAPTER 5: CHOOSING THE RIGHT VEGETABLES AND FRUITS

When you start thinking about and planning your container garden, you might already envision yourself enjoying a meal filled with your favorite vegetables organically grown in your garden. Or, enjoy a deliciously sweet strawberry freshly picked from your container. However, as much as you probably can't wait to start planting, it's important that you take some time to consider whether the crops you want to grow will thrive in a container.

If you plan to bring your containers inside during the cold winter months or live in a warm climate, seasonal planting considerations won't be as vital as when creating a traditional in-ground garden. However, there are still some factors you should always be aware of, which we'll discuss in this chapter. We'll also look at companion plants and the magical aid this can bring to the overall health of your garden and plants.

Selecting the Right Vegetables and Fruits

You might have already guessed that big vegetables such as pumpkins, squash, and corn won't do well in a container as they need extensive space either for the actual vegetable to grow or for the roots to develop. While you might still have to buy these at your local supermarket, there are many vegetables you can easily grow in a container, regardless of how limited your space might be. I would like to share my handy hack for choosing plants to grow in containers: Where possible, always go for the bush or small varieties of plants. These are often referred to as dwarf or compact plants, and since they don't typically grow as big as the original varieties, their roots need significantly less space to develop.

This doesn't mean you can't grow vegetables when you can't find dwarf varieties. Let's look at vegetables that typically thrive when grown in containers:

- **Baby potatoes:** If you can wait a long time to harvest your crops, baby potatoes can do well in a large container. Many varieties are also available that mature quicker than a typical potato's usual 120-day growing season.

- **Beans:** This green vegetable can easily grow in a container, whether you opt for vining or bush beans. If you opt for vining beans, ensure you secure sufficient support for your plant.

- **Broccoli and cauliflower:** The size of the broccoli or cauliflower head you grow will depend on the size of your container, but this vegetable typically thrives in a container.

- **Carrots:** If you want to grow small carrots, you can do so if your container is big enough. Make sure the depth of your container is double the size of the variety of carrots you hope to grow.

- **Eggplant:** You won't be able to grow record-breaking-sized eggplants in a container, but smaller varieties do well in containers. Just note that this vegetable is generally sensitive to cool temperatures, so bringing your container inside is best if you live in a cold climate.

- **Leafy greens:** Most leafy greens do extremely well in containers. These hardy plants can survive in sun, shade, and even colder temperatures.

- **Peas:** This vegetable typically grows vertically and can do well in containers. Just ensure you add enough supports and train them to vine up your supports.

- **Peppers and chilis:** You can easily spice up your food with delicious peppers and chilis straight from your container garden.

- **Radishes:** This vegetable can easily grow in relatively small containers and do very well indoors as well.

- **Tomatoes:** This is another plant that grows extremely well in a container, particularly if you opt for cocktail or plum tomatoes and allow them to vine up.

- **Zucchini squash and mini cucumbers:** Always opt for the bush varieties and spread the seeds or seedlings to allow sufficient space to grow. Trellis supports work very well for this type of vegetable.

While these are just a small sample of vegetables that typically do well in containers, the list of crops you can grow is endless. However, don't limit yourself to only growing vegetables. The following fruits can easily thrive in container gardens:

- **Blackberries:** Blackberries typically grow as compact plants that don't need much space. As a result, they are great options for container gardens. There are also many thornless varieties, making harvesting and pruning much easier.

- **Blueberries:** As with moth forms of berries, blueberries thrive in containers, particularly if you make the soil slightly acidic by adding peat moss to your potting soil.

- **Dwarf fig:** Many different dwarf varieties of figs can do extremely well in containers. These plants grow only between four and eight feet tall and three feet wide, so adding them to a big pot in full sun can make a great addition to your garden.

- **Dwarf peach:** Similar to the dwarf fig, you can grow dwarf peaches easily in a container. Depending on the variety you choose, these plants typically mature to only about six feet in height.

- **Lemon:** Traditional lemon trees can grow very big with extensive root systems. However, many small varieties can do extremely well in bigger containers.

- **Passion fruit:** This tropical fruit does well in containers but can be sensitive to colder temperatures, so it's best to bring it indoors during the winter months.

- **Pineapple:** When you think of fruits to grow in a container, you might not immediately think of pineapples. However, if you cut the crown off a pineapple to plant, it can happily grow in a relatively small container. This tropical fruit also does extremely well indoors on a sunny windowsill.

- **Pomegranate:** Like lemon trees, pomegranates are typically too big for containers. Luckily, there are several dwarf cultivars available that can do well in pots on patios.

- **Strawberries:** This delicious berry can be grown in just about any type of container, including hanging baskets. Just make sure you don't overcrowd your containers with strawberry plants, as this can limit fruit production.

- **Watermelon:** You probably wouldn't have thought that you could successfully grow watermelon in a container. Unless you place your container in a big, open space, traditional watermelons would last too long. Luckily, there are smaller cultivars, such as the sugar baby bush watermelon, which don't vine longer than around three feet. If you choose to grow this type of fruit, make sure you use a fertilizer that's low in nitrogen but high in phosphorous, as nitrogen can limit the growth of fruit, as we'll discuss in Chapter 8.

Whether you plant seeds or seedlings (as we'll discuss in the next chapter), always make sure you follow the instructions on the packaging to ensure you plant them in the right season and allow the plant enough space to thrive.

Seasonal Planting Guide

You may already know that spring is the optimal time for a garden to develop and plant your new shrubs. If you have an indoor garden that can bring your plants inside during cold months or live in a climate without major temperature fluctuations, seasonal planting may be less of an issue than in traditional in-ground gardens. However, it's still important that you are aware of how seasonal changes may affect your garden. Let's look at the different seasons and how you should adjust your planting accordingly:

- **Spring:** During spring, your soil will warm up, regardless of whether you have a traditional in-ground or container garden. This is the time when your garden will naturally come to life, with new plants emerging and existing plants blooming. Depending on the climate in which you stay, spring can often be divided into three mini-seasons:

    - **Early spring:** These are the first few days or weeks of spring when temperatures can fluctuate between being very cold and getting warmer. If you live in a cold climate and your container garden is outside, your soil may likely be too hard to work properly. Wait until your soil can easily be managed before you plant your seeds or seedlings. If you find your soil dries quickly or remains hard, watering it more frequently can help. Adding a layer of mulch or compost on top of your soil can also be great in preparing your soil before you add your plants.

    - **Two weeks before the frost-free date:** Your frost-free date is when any frost in your area will likely be done for the season. We'll discuss how to determine the frost date in your area. Once you have this date, you can work about two weeks after this date. This is a good time to start acclimatizing your plants that can handle colder temperatures, such as leafy greens. You can do this by placing your seedlings outside for a few hours daily before you plant them in your containers.

- **Post frost-free date:** Once the threat of frost in your area has passed, you can start planting your seeds and seedlings. However, always check the specific needs of the plants you want to grow to ensure you grow them during the optimal times.

- **Summer:** When you reach the warm summer months, your fear of frost will be well behind you, and your plants should be thriving. However, if you live in a very hot climate, you should make sure your plants don't suffer from overheating. It's also not ideal to transplant seedlings in extreme heat, which can distress your plant and its root system. Some tips for gardening during the summer months include:

    - **Plant at the beginning of summer:** The early weeks of summer will likely be cooler than at the peak of the season, so it's best to make sure your summer annuals are planted during this time.

    - **Water well during hot months:** Your soil will dry out quicker during hot summer months, even if your container garden is inside or in the shade. We'll discuss tips on watering your garden in Chapter 9.

    - **Create a moat:** To ensure the water reaches your plant's roots, you can create a moat around your plant, which will help direct the moisture you add to your soil straight to your plant.

- **Fall:** By fall, you can start to prepare your garden for the cold winter months. If you have any expired seasonal plants, you can remove them from your containers to prepare your soil for the next season. If you can, you should now consider bringing your containers indoors. Depending on the type of plants you grow, your harvesting of fruits and vegetables should either come to an end or decrease in volume. Important gardening steps during the fall include:

- Clean your soil: As we've mentioned, this is a good time to remove any plants that are seasonal and have run their harvesting course. Then, remove any weeds and dead plant matter there might be in your containers.

- **Nourish your soil:** Once you've removed any old plant matter from your containers, you can work your soil to replace the nutrients your plants might have depleted over the previous season. This can help you reuse your soil during the following season so that you don't have to replace it every year.

- **Add your fall plants:** If you want to grow plants that bloom in spring and are hardy to cold temperatures, you can do so while the soil is still warm enough for root systems to develop. It's best to do so at least six weeks before the first frost is expected.

- **Winter:** Unless you have many annual plants or you bring your container garden inside during colder months, gardening in the winter entails more maintenance than actual gardening. If you're gardening seasonal plants, this is a fantastic time to rework your potting soil and add valuable ingredients and compost, as we discussed in the previous two chapters. If you have annual plants and you can't bring your containers inside, you should take the necessary precautions to keep them safe against cold temperatures and frost, which include:

  - **Manage your soil temperature:** Even though the soil in your containers will be somewhat protected against major temperature fluctuations, it's still important to manage your soil during these months. You can do this by adding a thick layer of mulch on top of your garden to insulate your soil.

  - **Avoid soil shifting:** While this is a bigger problem with traditional in-ground gardens, it can also be a factor in container gardening, especially if you use big pots. Soil shifting happens when your soil freezes and cracks during thawing. This can negatively affect your plant's roots. Again, adding mulch can help protect your soil from freezing and shifting.

- **Protect your plants from snow:** If you live in an area with a lot of snow and you can't bring your containers indoors, you need to protect your plants. Snow piles accumulating on your leaves can not only result in your plants freezing, but the weight can also break your branches. If it's snowing, you should regularly check your plants and gently knock off any snow that might be accumulating. Always start from the bottom and work your way up and then again down. This will prevent the bottom branches from accumulating even more snow than what already fell on them.

Understanding your climate and frost dates is very important if you live in a cold climate and want to grow annual plants outside. This is fairly simple: Your first frost date refers to the first day in winter that frost is expected in your area, while the last frost date is the day that frost is expected to clear. These dates are very important to help you take the necessary steps to avoid frost damage to your plants and plan when you should plant your seeds and seedlings to give them the best chance to thrive. However, since it's impossible to accurately predict the weather, you'll have to work on estimates based on your area's historical frost data. This will show you when frost is typically expected in your area. Then, for at least two weeks before frost is typically expected in your area, you should keep a close eye on weather forecasts to plan your garden accordingly.

While you have information on what you can expect in your gardening during all four seasons, you might still feel unsure of exactly how to plan planting your crops. After spending years documenting my plants' growth and harvesting, I created the following chart, which can help make your gardening journey much easier. Use the weeks from seed to harvesting as a guideline to work back to determine when you should plant your crops:

Name of plant:	**Height of mature plant:**	**Spacing per square foot:**	**Harvesting season:**	**Weeks from seed to harvest:**	**Seed storage:**
Basil	1 to 2 in	1 to 4	Summer	12	2 years
Beans	Bush: 12 to 18 in Pole: 7 to 9 ft	8 to 10	Summer	3 to 4	2 years
Beets	12 in	9	Spring to fall	8	4 to 5 years
Bok choy	1 to 2 ft	4	fall	6 to 7	4 years
Broccoli	18 to 24 in	1	Spring to fall	16	5 to 6 years
Brussels sprouts	2 to 3 ft	1	Spring to fall	20	4 years
Cabbage	12 to 18 in	1	Spring to fall	16	5 to 6 years
Carrots	12 in	1	Spring to fall	10	3 to 4 years
Cauliflower	18 to 24 in	1	Spring to fall	14	5 to 6 years
Celery	12 to 16 in	4	Spring to fall	12 to 14	4 to 5 years

Name of plant:	Height of mature plant:	Spacing per square foot:	Harvesting season:	Weeks from seed to harvest:	Seed storage:
Chives	6 to 12 in	16	Late spring and summer	16	2 years
Cilantro	1 to 2 ft	1	Late spring and summer	5	2 years
Collard greens	2 to 3 ft	1	Spring to winter	8 to 10	6 years
Cucumber	vine	2	Summer	9	5 to 6 years
Dill	3 ft	1	Summer	5	4 to 5 years
Eggplant	24 to 30 in	1	Summer	19	5 to 6 years
Fennel	30 to 72 in	1	Spring to fall	6	5 to 6 years
Garlic	18 to 24 in	9	Summer to fall	12	1 year
Kale	10 to 24 in	1	Spring to fall	6	4 years
Kohlrabi	12 to 18 in	9	Spring to fall	4 to 5	3 years

Name of plant:	Height of mature plant:	Spacing per square foot:	Harvesting season:	Weeks from seed to harvest:	Seed storage:
Leaf lettuce	6 to 12 in	4	Spring, fall, and winter	7	5 to 6 years
Leeks	24 in	9	Fall	14	2 years
Mint	1 to 3 in	1	Summer	3	1 year
Mustard greens	20 to 24 in	16	Spring and fall	4	4 years
Okra	18 to 24 in	1	Summer	12	2 years
Onions	12 in	16	Summer and fall	20	1 to 2 years
Oregano	1 to 2 ft	1	Spring to fall	16	1 year
Parsley	6 to 12 in	4	Spring to winter	14	2 to 3 years
Parsnips	10 to 15 in	4	Fall	15 to 17	1 year
Peas	Vine	8	Spring and fall	10	3 to 4 years
Peppers	12 to 24 in	4	Summer	19	4 to 5 years

Name of plant:	Height of mature plant:	Spacing per square foot:	Harvesting season:	Weeks from seed to harvest:	Seed storage:
Potatoes	12 to 24 in	4	Spring to fall	12	not applicable
Radishes	6 to 12 in	16	Spring to fall	4	5 to 6 years
Spinach	6 to 12 in	9	Spring, fall, and winter	7	5 to 6 years
Strawberries	6 to 12 in	4	Spring and fall	5	2 years
Swiss chard	12 to 18 in	4	Spring to winter	8	4 to 5 years
Tomatoes	Bush: 3 ft Vine: 6 ft	1 bush per 4 squares	Summer	17	4 to 5 years
Zucchini squash	Vine	1 per 2 squares	Summer	8	5 to 6 years

The Magic of Companion Planting

Now that you have a better idea of the vegetables and fruit you want to grow, and how you should consider your climate and seasonal changes, let's look at the magic of companion planting. This is the practice of specifically placing specific plants next to each other to benefit your garden. For example, if you plant nectar-rich flowers close to tomatoes, it can improve the insect pollination of your tomato plant.

When you create these growing communities of plants, your garden will gain many benefits, making your gardening journey a lot easier. Some of these benefits include:

- **Deter pests:** While you can spray pesticides on your garden to get rid of pests, these chemicals can harm your plants, especially if you want to eat your crops. Pesticides will also kill beneficial insects, which can hamper your plants' reproduction and fruit development. Luckily, many plants deter these pests, and if you plant them close to your precious vegetable plants, you can protect your crops without having to use pesticides.

- **Attract beneficial insects:** In the same way companion plants can deter pests, they can also attract beneficial insects, such as pollinating bees and pest-eating wasps.

- **Shade management:** If you want to create more shade for your plants, you can plant bigger plants next to them.

- **Plant support**: If you place a bigger plant next to your vining plants, you can train your vines to grow up your bigger plan to create natural supports for your vining plants.

- **Nutrient absorption:** All plants' nutritional needs are different and will absorb different nutrients from the soil. If you place plants with different nutritional needs together in the same soil, you can ensure both plants will gain everything they may need from the soil.

- **Weed suppression:** If you place sprawling plants, such as potatoes, next to upright plants, the sprawling plants can provide a soil covering similar to what mulch will offer and can suppress the growth of weeds.

Now that you understand how companion planting can make your gardening journey much easier and greatly benefit your plants, let's look at how you can do this. If these plans weren't already on your list of plants you want to grow:

- **Basil:** If you plan to grow tomatoes, have a few basil plants nearby. Basil repels many pests, such as moths and thrips, that can affect the fruits of your tomato plants. Basil also lures bees, which will improve the pollination of your tomato plant.

- **Borage:** This is another herb that goes well with tomatoes, and strawberries.

- **Dill**: This herb attracts ladybugs, a beneficial insect that eats many garden pests.

- **Garlic:** Much like the vegetable, this plant has a strong smell that repels many insects, including aphids, ermine moths, and onion flies. This plant is excellent to use between potatoes, cabbages, and leafy greens.

- **Mint:** This herb's strong smell deters many pests, including flea beetles, ants, and aphids. If you decide to grow mint, make sure you plant it in a separate container, as this herb is a very aggressive grower that can easily take over your entire garden.

- **Nasturtiums:** This flower lures caterpillars away from brassicas, such as kale, broccoli, and cabbage, and black flies from beans.

- **Parsley:** This herb also attracts beneficial insects and bees for the pollination of your vegetable flowers.

- **Poached egg plants:** This wildflower (not the vegetable) attracts the beneficial insect hoverflies. This insect controls the spread of aphids, especially if planted close to lettuce.

- **Sage:** This is another excellent herb to add to your vegetable garden, as it repels carrot flies and cabbage moths.

- **Sunflowers:** While this flower will bring beautiful color to your garden, it also repels many pests. What's more, due to their long stems, they provide excellent support for climbing and vining plants, such as cucumbers and beans.

- **Tansy:** This flowering plant attracts many pest-eating bugs, such as predatory wasps and ladybugs. It's also known to repel cutworms, which can destroy many different vegetables, including tomatoes, potatoes, peppers, peas, lettuce, cabbage, carrots, beans, celery, and asparagus.

You're now just about ready to start placing your plants. You know what fruit and vegetables grow well in containers, and what companion plants will help your garden thrive. Now, you're probably left with a big question: How do I plant my crops? Do I grow them from seeds or take the shortcut to plant seedlings? These questions will be answered in the next chapter.

CHAPTER 6: SEEDS VERSUS SEEDLINGS: MAKING THE RIGHT CHOICE

I remember when I started my first garden and how confused I felt during my trip to my local nursery. Apart from not knowing what soil to buy or how to add (or make) compost, I was left with another big question. I knew exactly what vegetables and fruit I wanted to grow, but I soon realized it wasn't as simple as that. In the nursery, there were many options for seeds and seedlings at various stages of growth. Asking the sales assistant didn't help much, as he just shrugged his shoulders, telling me it was a personal choice. Confused, I left without buying anything. I went home to research seeds and seedlings, and after carefully considering the benefits and disadvantages of each one, I felt more comfortable and confident in making a decision.

If you're feeling just as confused as I was, we'll now discuss the differences between seeds and seedlings and the pros and cons of each of them. We'll also look at tips on how you can grow your seeds indoors so that weather conditions and climate don't affect your seeds, and how you can transplant your seedlings without disrupting their root systems.

Difference Between Seeds and Seedlings

Before we go into the benefits and disadvantages of each of these, let's first look at what exactly is meant by seeds and seedlings:

- **Seed:** A seed is an embryonic plant with a hard, protective outer coating, called the seed coat. Plants are grown by planting seeds in the soil. Water and temperature are then added to start a process called germination, where the seed coat breaks open and a tiny plant emerges. However, if the seeds are planted too thickly, it can hamper germination. Also, if it's planted too deep in the soil, it can reduce the amount of airflow to the seed, halting this process again. It's generally recommended that seeds be planted at about double the depth of the actual seed.

- **Seedling:** A seedling is a young plant grown from a seed in a nursery. They are typically sold in trays of six to eight seedlings, which you can then transplant straight into your garden.

As you can guess, there is no right or wrong answer to whether you should grow your garden from seeds or seedlings; both options have definite pros and cons that should be considered before you decide. If you've never handled seeds before, it can be easier for beginner gardeners to start their gardens with seedlings, especially if you can get these young plants that have matured to more than four inches in length. This way, you only have to worry about making sure your seedling doesn't die instead of worrying about creating the right environment for germination to take place. Alternatively, if you want to grow your garden for seeds (and trust me, there is no better feeling than eating a vegetable you've grown from a tiny seed), I suggest you start with beans, as these are probably the easiest seeds to grow.

The Pros and Cons of Planting Seeds

Let's now look at growing seeds and things you need to consider when deciding whether you want to try your hand at becoming a germination expert:

- **Pros of growing from seeds**
    - Seeds are significantly cheaper than seedlings, and since you can keep leftover seeds for months (if not years), you can potentially get a few seasons out of a single packet of seeds.
    - There are a huge variety of different seeds available for you to germinate. While your local nursery will have rows and rows of packets of seeds, you can also order seeds online. This means you can grow vegetables that aren't native to your area or even your country.
    - Many crops, such as beans, will germinate within a few days, so you'll have your first vegetables ready for harvesting within a few weeks.

- If you plant your seeds directly into the container you wish to grow your vegetables in, you won't risk any damage to your plant's roots when transplanting them.

- **Cons of growing from seeds**

    - Direct seeding can be trickier and riskier than transplanting a seedling. Unless you grow your seeds indoors, you'll have to account for weather conditions, which include rain and high wind, which can blow the soil off your seed and expose it to the elements, which will stop the germination process.

    - If there are any weeds, bacteria, pests, or diseases in your soil, it can contaminate your seed and hamper the germination process.

    - It can be difficult to know when you're overseeing. If you don't give your seeds enough space to develop, germination won't be successful, as your seeds will have to compete for nutrients, water, and light. Crowded seeds are also more susceptible to disease as there won't be proper airflow to them.

    - Growing from seeds adds at least a few weeks to your gardening season. If you live in a short spring and summer climate, your plants might not have enough time to properly develop and mature. This can be particularly tricky if you grow vegetables that germinate slowly. However, you can minimize this by starting your seeds indoors during the winter months, as we'll discuss in the next section.

Leafy greens, radishes, turnips, baby beetroot, peas, beans, zucchini squash, spring onions, and broccoli are vegetables that typically grow fast from seeds, and you may be able to harvest your first crops within two months of planting your seeds. If you're an impatient gardener or desperate to enjoy your first homegrown crops, these are good options to start with.

Root vegetables, like onions, carrots, and beetroot, generally don't transplant well. If you aren't careful handling these, you can disturb your plants so badly that your crop may be deformed. With these vegetables, growing them directly from seeds can be more beneficial..

Growing Seeds Successfully Indoors

Growing your own fruit and vegetables from seeds is a gateway to leading a sustainable and fulfilling way of life. With the rising cost of living, more and more people are turning to growing their own produce from seeds. My first foray into planting seeds was a mixed bag. I started with lettuce seeds, and when they started sprouting in no time, I felt emboldened to try tomatoes, watermelons, and peas. The peas had about a 50% success rate but the tomatoes and watermelons just never took hold. My biggest mistake was not having the right environment for them to thrive. I tried to grow too many seeds, so not all got enough sunlight. Since I pared my efforts back to planting just two or three different seed varieties each month, I have had much more success with growing seeds.

If you follow these few basic steps, you can be successful in growing most types of seeds indoors:

- Choose the container you want to grow your seeds in. While you can use small buckets and then transplant your seedlings, I found that it's best to grow your seeds directly into the container you want to use for your mature plants, as this will eliminate you having to handle them and disrupt their roots.

- Place your container in a warm area with proper lighting for your seeds to germinate. Windowsills work excellently for this purpose. If you don't want your windowsills to be full of pots, you can use grow lights and even a heat mat to ensure your seeds can germinate in a warm environment.

- Fill your containers with good potting soil. Refer back to Chapter 3 for tips on selecting and augmenting your soil.

- Make sure your soil is moist before you plant them. When you plant your seeds, make sure they are placed around double to three times the depth of your seed. Refer to the instructions on the seed packaging for the spatial requirements for placing your seeds.

- Check your soil daily to make sure it doesn't dry out. You can gently touch your soil. If it feels moist, you can leave it as is. If it's at all dry to the touch, you can gently add water. When watering seeds, I found it best to use a spray bottle, as you won't run the risk of flooding your seeds or disturbing the soil covering your seeds.

- Before you move your plants outdoors, you can prepare them for the elements outside by hardening them off. This is the process of taking them out for a few hours daily.

A package of seeds will usually contain instructions on how and when you should plant your seeds, such as "Start indoors eight weeks before the last expected frost date in your area." As discussed in the previous chapter, a simple internet search will tell you the date of the expected last frost in your area. Count backward to, for example, eight weeks before that, and that's more or less the date you should start your seeds. Other things to consider include:

- **Planting time:** Most seed packets will tell you quite clearly if the seeds can or should be started indoors. For some species (tomatoes, for example), starting seeds indoors in cold-weather climates is virtually mandatory. For other species, it may be optional. However, if you plant your seeds directly in the containers you wish to grow your plants in, you can start it anywhere. Move your container outdoors once your plants have matured sufficiently.

- **Days to maturity:** This will tell you how long the plants take to produce edible fruit, vegetables, or ornamental flowers. Some tomato plants take as much as 100 days to reach fruit-producing maturity. If you want tomatoes in July, this means the seeds need to be started in early April.

- **Light needs:** The seed package will tell you if the seeds need lots of light. If so, starting them indoors may require a fluorescent grow light—or, as we've mentioned, you may need to reserve your sunniest window for seed-starting.

- **Soil needs:** Some seeds can be started in ordinary potting soil, while others require a porous, fine-grained seed-starting mix. The package may also suggest an optimal soil temperature for seeds to germinate. Seeds that require 70-degree soil to germinate must be started indoors in cold-weather climates since the soil does not get adequately warm until late into May (depending on where you stay, obviously).

The Benefits and Disadvantages of Seedlings

Now, let's turn our attention to growing your garden from seedlings. As mentioned, these are young plants that have been grown in a nursery or by a farmer and have matured enough to be transplanted into your garden, be it a traditional in-ground or container garden.

- **Benefits of seedlings**

    - Transplanting seedlings into your garden gives you a head start in your growing season, as they will generally mature quickly and provide you with edible vegetables and fruits quicker than growing from seeds.

    - Since seedlings have reached some level of maturity, they will be more resistant to disease and pests.

    - Unless you're an experienced gardener, caring for a seedling is a much easier process than germinating a seed. Harvesting your first crop from seedlings can give you the boost in confidence you may need on your gardening journey.

- **Disadvantages of seedlings**
    - Seedlings are significantly more expensive than buying a packet of seeds. However, since your chances of success will be higher with seedlings than with seeds, spending extra on seedlings might be worth your buck, especially if you're a newbie gardener.
    - The available variety of seedlings will be a lot less than with seeds. You can't simply order seedlings online as you can with seeds, so you're limited with what your local suppliers have in stock.
    - Unless you buy your seedlings from a highly reputable and certified producer, you may risk introducing disease to your garden. Although this risk will be more confined in a container garden than a traditional in-ground garden, it's still something you should always consider.

Besides root vegetables and crops with extensive root systems, such as beans, most fruit, and vegetables grow well from seedlings. You have to, however, make sure you take the necessary care when you transplant your seedlings to ensure you don't disturb the root systems.

Transplanting Seedlings to Containers

Even though transplanting seedlings from the trays into your containers is a relatively easy process, it's important that you do this gently. Remember, even though these plants have reached some level of maturity, they are still young, delicate plants that can easily break. If it's possible, it's best to transplant your seedlings early in the morning on a warm, overcast, windless day. This way, your plant will have time to settle before being exposed to the midday sun or strong winds. Other steps you can take include:

- Decide on a container you want to use for your plant. Remember, when you're transplanting your seedling, you'll move it to its new, permanent location, so the container you choose will be the one your plant will remain in.

- Fill your container with soil, and make sure you add enough moisture to it. It shouldn't be too wet or too dry. If you feel unsure of what the moisture level should be, you can wet your soil deeply the previous day and allow it to drain the next day.

- Dig a hole that's slightly bigger than the depth of the tray your seedling came in. This will help you make sure you plant your seedling at the right depth in your container.

- Loosen your seedling from the tray. You can use a butter knife or a hand trowel to loosen the soil from the sides of the tray.

- Gently grip your plant's stem between your thumb and index finger, but don't pull your plant out. Instead, turn your tray upside down and let the plant, with the soil surrounding the roots, fall into your hand. If it doesn't come out immediately, you can tap the bottom of the tray to get it out.

- Place your seedling with the surrounding soil into your container and fill any holes between the seedling's soil and your container hole with soil. You can gently tamp down the soil to ensure proper contact with the seedling's soil.

- Water your seedling immediately after you transplant it to eliminate air pockets and assist the roots in settling in their new environment. Over the next few days, keep a close eye on your soil to ensure it stays moist. If you live in a dry climate, you can spread mulch as a top layer over the soil to boost moisture retention.

After you transplant your seedlings, it can be beneficial to keep your container indoors for a few days to ensure your plant is protected from the elements while it's adapting to its new environment. Then, go through the process of hardening your seedling off before you move it to its permanent location outside.

Whether you keep your container garden permanently inside or move it outdoors, as discussed above, you should inspect your plants frequently to check for any signs of pests or disease. In the next chapter, we'll discuss the most common pests found in container gardens and organic remedies to get rid of them.

CHAPTER 7: ORGANIC PEST REMEDIES

When you spend some time observing your garden, you might be surprised at the vast amount of insects and bugs crawling around your plant. But did you know that some of these insects may actually be beneficial for your garden and may give your plants the boost they may need to grow optimal crops? However, you may have no idea which of these are harmful to your plants and should be removed and which might help your garden thrive.

Getting rid of pests can also pose many more questions. Your local nursery will likely stock many different pesticides, with many of them containing chemicals that may be harmful, to your plants and yourself if you eat your crops. Luckily, there are many organic remedies you can safely use for pest control, which include sprays you can easily make at home, as well as using beneficial companion plants.

To help you with this important step in your gardening journey, we'll now discuss how you can identify some of the most common pests in your garden, how you can get rid of them in a natural, safe manner, and which insects are beneficial for your garden.

Identifying Common Pests

For insects, your beautiful garden can seem like a massive buffet of delicious food that they can feed on. Unfortunately, this will cause extensive damage to your garden. You may suddenly see brown spots on your green leaves, bite marks on your crops, and even insect eggs accumulating on your plants. Unfortunately, the visible evidence of pests you can see in your garden is typically only the tip of the iceberg, which is why it's so important to frequently inspect your garden and take the necessary action whenever you see even the tiniest signs of unwanted creatures crawling around.

Identifying pests in your garden comes down to either seeing the insects or the damage they cause to your plants and crops. Some of the most common pests you might find in your garden include:

- **Aphids:** These are small pear-shaped insects that can come in various colors. Depending on their coloration, they are often referred to as black or green flies. They suck the juices of many types of vegetables, such as kale, cabbage, lettuce, and tomatoes. While you may see the actual insects flying or crawling around your garden, other signs can be stunted, curling, or yellowing leaves. Always look at the bottom of your leaves, as aphids often hide there. If you find any aphids in your garden, you can use dish soap and water to spray your plants.

- **Asparagus beetle:** These bugs are black with yellow spots on their backs and a red mark on their heads. As the name suggests, they prefer feeding on asparagus plants, turning the leaves brown. You may also see small eggs on your plants, which you should remove and squash. These bugs will remain in your soil throughout the cold winter months, so it's important to properly treat your soil should you have an infestation in your garden.

- **Cabbage worms:** If your cabbage leaves are full of holes, you most likely have cabbage worms in your garden. These are green caterpillars with a line on their backs. As the name suggests, they love feeding on cabbage leaves but can also be a problem for your broccoli, brussels sprouts, cauliflower, radish, kale, and turnips. Inspect your plants closely, and remove the worms from your garden. You can remove any worms you see. Also, check the leaves for eggs and spray them off using an apple cider vinegar mixture, which we'll discuss below.

- **Carrot fly:** These tiny black flies have orange legs and heads and feed on many different vegetables, including carrots, parsley, celery, and parsnips. The fly's beige-colored maggot larvae feed on the roots of the plants. Since these flies are weak flyers, you can place your container in a windy area or plant them close to other plants with strong scents, as this smell will repel these flies.

- **Colorado potato beetle:** These are tiny red beetles with black stripes on their backs. They typically feed on many vegetables that grow well in containers, such as peppers, tomatoes, eggplants, and potatoes, as well as the leaves of these plants. These pests remain in the soil throughout the year, so if you struggle with this type of beetle during the season, you should take extra care over the winter months to treat your soil. Neem-based organic sprays, which we'll discuss below, can work well against this type of pest.

- **Cutworms:** These are yellow, green, brown, or grey caterpillars of brown or grey moths. They typically feed on the outer stem of cabbage, broccoli, kale, or tomato plants and particularly prefer young, immature plants. You can protect your plants by sliding an empty toilet paper roll over their stems or covering them in foil.

- **Flea beetles:** These are tiny black or brown insects that feed on the leaves of radishes, tomatoes, brassicas, potatoes, and eggplants. Their larvae will feel on the roots of these plants. Garlic oil can be a very effective repellent against these bugs.

- **Leafminers:** While these pests don't feed on the plant itself, their green or brown larvae mine inside the plant tissue of spinach, beets, blueberries, and Swiss chard. If you ever see tunnels forming in your plants, you prune the leaves immediately to prevent further damage to your plant.

- **Slugs and snails:** Not many people don't know what these slimy creatures look like. You can typically easily tell if you have slugs and snails in your garden, not just by the physical creature but also by the shiny residue they leave behind and holes eaten from your plant's leaves. When I first set up my container garden, I would find plant leaves had served as something's dinner. One of the best things I found to protect my plants was to crush eggshells and place them over the top of the soil. This created a sharp barrier that would deter the snails and slugs from getting close to my plants.

- **Squash bugs:** These are oval-shaped, dark brown bugs that are commonly found in vegetable gardens. The most obvious sign of a squash bug infestation is damaged leaves that turn yellow and crisp. Since these bugs typically remain close to the ground, creating vertical gardens can help reduce them. Always check the bottom of your plant's leaves for eggs. Sticky tape can be a very effective tool to remove these eggs.

- **Tomato hornworms:** These are green caterpillars with white stripes over their bodies and horns on their heads. They typically feed on tomatoes, potatoes, eggplants, and peppers. During the day, they will normally hide underneath the leaves, feeding at night. If you ever see these worms in your garden, you can simply hand-remove them.

- **Whiteflies:** These are small, white flies that leave a sticky residue on your plants. You'll often see them at the bottom of the leaves of citrus trees, tomatoes, and peppers. Hanging yellow sticky cards close to your plants can lure these flies away from your garden.

Recipe for Neem Oil

Regarding natural pesticides, neem oil provides an excellent option as it's inexpensive, non-toxic to both pets and humans, and gives long-term solutions against pests in your garden. This oil is an evergreen tree endemic to India. It's an excellent repellent against pests like aphids and whiteflies.

While you can buy a great variety of neem oil sprays at your local nursery, making these at home is also very easy. In fact, creating a DIY neem oil spray can be beneficial, as you can adjust the concentration levels according to the level of infestation in your garden. Making it yourself is usually also far cheaper in the long run than buying already-made sprays. This is my favorite recipe for neem oil spray:

- Ensure you use a good-quality 100% neem oil or neem leaf extract. This is often called raw neem or crude oil. It's best to buy oils that have been cold-pressed, as this will reduce the risk of your oil being contaminated.

- Just like any other oil, neem oil won't mix with water, so you'll have to first emulsify it using a mild liquid soap. You can add a few drops of soap to your oil.

- Next, you can create your spray by mixing a liter of water, a few drops of dish soap, and a teaspoon of neem oil together.

- Pour this mixture into a spray bottle and use it within eight hours, as the ingredients may start to break down if stored for longer.

Recipe for Apple Cider Vinegar Spray

Another non-toxic homemade spray that can be very effective as a pesticide is made from apple cider vinegar. Due to its low acid content, this spray can even help fertilize your plants and soil while you're working on getting rid of your pests. You can also use this mixture to clean any buildup on your plant's leaves and gardening equipment by spraying some on a soft cloth and gently wiping your levels and equipment after use. The smell of this vinegar on your plant's leaves can also help repel pests from your garden.

Making apple cider vinegar spray is as easy as mixing water and vinegar in a spray bottle. If you want, you can add a few drops of lemon juice to this mixture; however, this isn't entirely necessary.

Companion Planting for Pest Control

Just as companion planting can help your different plants gain the maximum nutritional benefits from the soil, it can also go a long way in deterring pests from your garden. While we've already mentioned some of these in the previous chapter, let's focus now on how companion planting can be a fantastic pest control method.

As you'll see on the list below, herbs are extremely beneficial plants to not only chase away pests but also attract pollinators. Let's look at some of the pests you might find in your garden and the herbs you can consider adding to your garden:

- **Ants**: Tansy and bay leaves.
- **Aphids**: Marigolds, cilantro, basil, and catmint.
- **Beetles**: Rose-scented geranium.
- **Cabbage fly**: Celery, garlic, cilantro, and rose-scented geranium.
- **Fruit flies**: Marigolds and tansy.
- **Flies**: Lemon verbena, basil, and catmint.
- **Fleas**: Fennel, catmint, and Khakibos.
- **Mosquitoes**: Lemon verbena.
- **Snails and cutworms:** Oak leaves and mustard.
- **Tomato hornworm**: Borage.
- **Whiteflies**: Marigolds.

Apart from these more specific companions, many other plants can do extremely well at deterring pests from your garden. As a rule of thumb, any plant with a strong smell, such as lavender, santolina, elder, and feverfew, can do well to boost your container garden.

Beneficial Insects for Your Plants

Just as not all plants will bring the same benefits to your garden, not all bugs are created equally. While you might believe that you should try to repel all insects from your garden, some can play an important role in a healthy, thriving garden. This is because they can improve pollination in the flowers of your fruits and vegetables, but they can also chase harmful pests away from your garden.

Let's look at five insects you really want to have in your garden:

- **Bees:** As you may know, bees serve a vital role in pollinating all fruits, vegetables, and flowers. The more bees you can have in your garden, the more bountiful your harvests will likely be. You can attract bees to your garden by planting bright-colored flowers such as asters, zinnias, daisies, or herbs like mint and oregano close to your garden.

- **Ground beetles:** These are predatory beetles that eat other insects, their larvae, and pests like slugs and caterpillars. Nectar-rich plants are great attractors for ground beetles.

- **Ladybugs:** These bugs feed on aphids. You can attract this insect to your garden by planting flat-topped flowers such as angelica, as well as herbs such as dill and fennel.

- **Praying mantises:** These green insects feed on many bad bugs, such as aphids, flies, and crickets. Marigolds, raspberries, dill, and fennel are great at luring praying mantises to your garden.

- **Spiders:** Although you might think of spiders as pests, they can be helpful in your garden as they hunt other insects for food. Having spiders in your garden will also help attract birds, who may eat other harmful pests.

As your garden develops and thrives, you should always keep an eye on the state of your soil to ensure the nutrition your plants need doesn't get depleted. This can include testing your soil and adding organic fertilizers when necessary. We'll discuss this, as well as how to avoid overfertilizing, in the next chapter.

CHAPTER 8: ORGANIC NUTRIENT MANAGEMENT

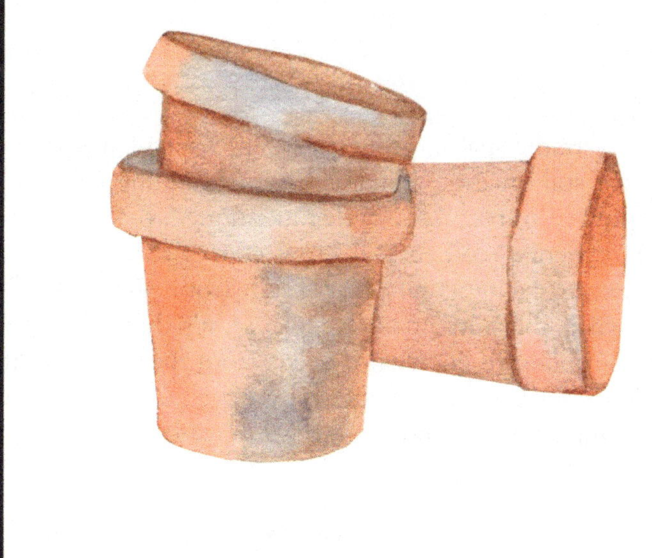

Just when your garden starts to thrive and you can start to harvest your crops, you may have to deal with a new problem: nutrient depletion in your garden. Every day that your plant grows and you water your garden, you're depleting the goodness in your soil that your crop needs to thrive. Unfortunately, you can't just look at your soil or ask your plants if they have any needs that are unmet. Instead, you'll have to literally dig deep to test your soil and add organic fertilizer when necessary to feed your plants.

You should, however, ensure you never over-fertilize your garden, as this can bring a host of other problems to your garden and negatively affect the success of your harvests. Luckily, you can reduce overcomplicating this important aspect of gardening, in many ways, as we'll discuss in this chapter.

Understanding Nutritional Needs of Container Plants

When you have a traditional in-ground garden, your plant's roots will expand to unused soil once the immediately surrounding soil has been depleted of important nutrients. As we've mentioned, this isn't the case with container gardening. When you grow your plants in pots, your roots are limited to gaining all their food from the soil in that container, and when the nutrients are depleted, it's done. There is no other way for your plant to get what it needs from the soil, even if you mix a slow-release fertilizer into your soil before adding your plants. This is why it's important to understand the nutritional needs of your plants.

While it's easy to go into a lot of scientific detail on this important topic, I'm going to simplify this as much as possible; if you want to know the very specifics on this, there is plenty of good information available online, which will likely be unnecessary for newbie gardeners. So, at the risk of oversimplifying it, the three essential nutrients your plants need include nitrogen (N), phosphorus (P), and potassium (K).

Secondary nutrients are calcium, magnesium, and sulfur, and micronutrients, such as iron, manganese, zinc, and others.

Unless you have an extensive soil tester kit, knowing exactly which nutrients are missing from your soil can be difficult. While this might not be a perfect science, my experience with gardening taught me to focus on what I want from my garden. If I want to extend my plant's growth and leaf production, I add nitrogen-rich fertilizer to my soil. If I want to boost my plant's production of fruits and vegetables, I opt for a fertilizer with higher amounts of potassium and phosphorus. Alternatively, if I want to improve the overall health of my garden, I go for a good all-purpose fertilizer. On the packaging of these, you'll see a 10-10-10 NPK. This basically means that it contains equal amounts of the three essential nutrients for your plants.

As a general rule of thumb, plants grown in containers may exhaust the available nutrients within around six weeks, regardless of the type and quality of potting soil or compost you use. This is, however, dependent on the rate at which your plant grows and your watering schedule. This is why it's so important that you keep a gardening diary so that you can know exactly when your plants have been growing for a month and start testing your soil to prevent nutrient depletion before your plant's important food runs out.

Apart from the composition of the fertilizer, you also have the option of using either a soluble one or slow-release pellets, a decision that will largely be dependent on your garden's specific needs. To help you decide, here are some important things to consider:

- Soluble fertilizers dissolve easily in water, allowing your plants' roots to gain access to them easily. You can throw the fertilizer powder straight onto your soil before watering your garden or first dissolve it in water. I found using hot water to work best to break it down before adding it to my soul.

- Soluble fertilizers are easy to use, especially in container gardens with limited space for soil, and digging in this soil to add fertilizer pellets may disrupt your plant's root system.

- If there are visible signs of nutrition depletion in your plant and you want to treat it quickly, soluble fertilizers are ideal.

- Slow-release fertilizer pellets are very helpful to use when you're starting a garden or before you add a plant to your container, as the fertilizer is released into the soil gradually through watering your garden.

- Slow-release fertilizer pellets are very convenient, especially if you're new to gardening and still learning about the needs of your soil and plants.

During my gardening journey, I made many mistakes in understanding my garden's fertilization needs. I'm sure most gardeners bump their heads a few times with this, as under fertilizing your garden can reduce the quality and quantity of your crops, while overfertilizing can damage your plants, as we'll discuss later. After a process of trial and error, I developed this three-step fertilizer plan for my container garden:

1. I add slow-release fertilizer pellets into my potting mix before I place new plants. However, since new potting soil is typically well-fertilized, this can easily result in overfertilization. To avoid this, I opt for very slow-release pellets with a thick polymer coating: the thicker the coating, the slower the fertilizer will release. Most fertilizers will also indicate an average release time on the packaging. While the average length of time for fertilizer release is around 60 days, some can last for up to 120 days. Unless my plant or soil has immediate needs, I need to attend to them, and I generally go for a 120-day release as a form of garden maintenance.

2. I started to test my soil around four weeks after planting my crops. As soon as I start seeing any signs of nutrient depletion, either through my tests or on my plants, I add soluble fertilizer to my soil. Here, I decide on the fertilizer composition according to what I believe my plants need, but as mentioned above, if you're unsure, you typically won't make a mistake by adding a 10-10-10 NPK all-purpose fertilizer. If you plant leafy greens, you can always use a nitrogen-rich fertilizer for foliage production.

3. If my plants ever seem stressed, which can often be the case during extreme heat, I spray a soluble fertilizer straight onto the leaves (top and bottom) after pruning away any old blooms or damaged foliage. This can give your plants the pick-me-up they may need to boost the process of photosynthesis.

Benefits of Organic Fertilizers

Now that you have a better idea of how fertilizers should be used, you have another choice to make between using synthetic or organic fertilizers:

- **Organic fertilizers:** These are made from natural products, such as herbs, seaweed, fish meal emulsion, liquid kelp, and animal manure, to name a few. They are very easy to use and typically won't damage your garden if you're overfertilizing. They work to improve the structure of your soil while stimulating the important microorganisms in it. While they typically have a lower NPK composition, their effect on your garden can be longer-lasting. Unfortunately, this can also mean that it will take longer after application before you see any changes in your garden, so if your plants need a quick pick-me-up, organic fertilizers might not work as effectively. They are typically more expensive than synthetic variants.

- **Synthetic fertilizers:** These come in either soluble powder or liquid or slow-release pellets that have been manufactured from minerals, gases, and inorganic waste materials and are often a lot cheaper than organic variants. They typically have a higher NPK composition, which can bring quick results to your plants. However, the results will be more short-term, and the fertilizer will have to be reapplied more frequently. Unfortunately, this poses the risk of overfertilizing your garden, which can burn your plants.

Understanding the differences between these two types of fertilizers might not be enough to convince you which one will be best for your garden. While you should opt for the one that best suits your budget, garden, and lifestyle, I highly recommend using organic fertilizers due to these benefits:

- **Improved biodiversity in your soil:** Using natural fertilizers can give microbiological activity in your soil a boost. Through this, organisms in your soil will break your organic fertilizer down into amino acids and humic acids, drawing air to your soil to make the soil structure lighter for your plants' roots to thrive. This improved biodiversity will also aid your plant in becoming more resistant to pests and diseases.

- **More fertile soil:** Apart from improving the soil structure, organic fertilizers will also bring more nutrients to your soil and boost the soil's ability to retain moisture. Organic fertilizers will also provide your crop with secondary nutrients and micronutrients, such as copper, calcium, zinc, magnesium, and sulfur. Very few synthetic fertilizers contain these nutrients.

- **Longer-lasting results:** As we've mentioned, the effects of organic fertilizers are typically longer-lasting than those of synthetic fertilizers. This is because nutrients are only released into the soil when bacteria break the organic pellets down, unlike water-diluting synthetic ones.

- **Environmentally friendly:** As you can probably guess, organic fertilizers are much friendlier to the environment than synthetically manufactured ones.

Simple Herb Fertilizer Recipe

While your local nursery will most likely stock a variety of organic fertilizers, you can use for your container garden, you can also easily make one yourself using herbs from your garden. In fact, even old, dried herbs in your spice rack, such as oregano, sage, and dill, can be added to your fertilizer. Other herbs you should definitely look at adding include comfrey (high in potassium, phosphorous, and magnesium), stinging nettle (rich in iron, sulfur, and magnesium), horsetail (which contains silica, which boosts your plant's overall health), and borage (loaded with many nutrients).

I would like to share my favorite (and super easy) recipe to create your own herb fertilizer at home:

- Chop your herbs roughly and place them into a bucket. You can use the entire herb (stem, leaves, and flowers). After you put them in the bucket, you can push them down slightly. This will aid the release of nutrients from these plants. I recommend making the bucket at least half full with plant matter.

- Fill your bucket to the top with water. You can use normal tap water, or you can speed up the process by using warm water. However, don't add boiling hot water to the mixture, as this might damage or kill the goodness you want to extract from the plant matter.

- Put your bucket in the sun and leave it to rest for at least a day. The longer you leave your concoction to brew, the stronger it will get. However, do remember that nitrogen-rich herbs such as comfrey and stinging nettle can become smelly if left too long. Make sure you cover it with either mesh or cloth to prevent mosquitoes or other insects from laying eggs in your mixture.

- Stir your mixture frequently during the day to add aeration to your mixture. This will give your soil and the organisms living in it the necessary boost to turn it into a nutrient-rich environment for your plants.

- Strain your herbs and pour your mixture into a spray bottle or watering can. It should look like weak tea. You can then add this mixture straight to your soil or use it on your plants' leaves to boost them. It's best applied early in the morning when the sun isn't intense, or late in the afternoon. If you see any signs of leaf burning (there shouldn't be), you can dilute this mixture by adding water.

Test Your Soil

Understanding the importance of using the right fertilizer for your garden is one thing, but knowing when your garden needs it can bring about a host of new questions and concerns. Your local nursery will likely sell extensive soil testing kits that can be extremely helpful in determining exactly what your garden needs. Most of these nurseries also offer a soil testing service, where you can take a sample of your soil for them to examine. They will look at the available nutrients in your soil and make recommendations on how you can create an optimal growing environment for your plants. Or, as mentioned above, you can also look at the condition of your plants to know when they need an extra boost.

Ultimately, apart from keeping track of the longevity of the fertilizers I add and when I plant my crop, I've found the most important aspect of this process is to ensure you have the right soil pH. This refers to the level of acidity in your soil and will directly impact your plant's absorption of nutrients. Again, at the risk of oversimplifying it:

- If your pH is too high, you will have alkaline soil. As a result, important nutrients such as phosphorus and iron may not be readily available to your plants. Ground sulfur can help treat alkaline soil.

- If your pH is too low, your soil is acidic, which can be toxic to your plants. It can stunt the development and health of roots, causing your plants to turn yellow. Adding finely ground limestone can help increase your soil's pH level.

A quick pantry test can also be very helpful to determine whether you have alkaline or acidic soil. However, remember that this test should be used as a baseline to determine the need for taking more extensive steps or doing further tests. I do this quick pantry test about once a month during the growing season or whenever I see any signs of depletion in my plants:

- Put about two tablespoons of soil in a bowl and add around half a cup of vinegar. If the mixture fizzes, your soil is likely alkaline.

- Place another two tablespoons of soil in a bowl and moisten it with sterile water. This will ensure that your test doesn't react to the chemicals in the water but only to your soil. Then, add around half a cup of baking soda. Again, if your mixture fizzes, your soil is acidic.

- If there is no reaction during either of these tests, your soil likely has a neutral pH level, and no further action should be required.

How to Avoid Over-Fertilization

Regardless of the fertilizer you choose, it's important that you take the necessary steps to avoid overfertilizing your garden. When this happens, you run the risk of damaging your plants all the way from the roots to the leaves. Testing your soil and following the instructions on the fertilizer label to ensure proper application. To be safe, it's best to go with a less-is-more approach. If the instructions call for one scoop of fertilizer per gallon of water, you can try half a scoop per gallon and fertilize more frequently.

When you overfertilize your garden, the chemicals (salts) in the fertilizer can damage the roots and their ability to absorb water from the soil. This can not only cause soil acidification, which will affect your plant's growth and fruit development, but also expose your plant to various root diseases that might be present in your soil. Conversely, overfertilization can also result in sudden plant growth without sufficient root development. In most cases, this will also ultimately result in your plant dying.

Some of the most common signs of overfertilization include:

- The fertilizer will form a crust on the surface of the soil.

- Your plant's leaves will turn yellow and start to wilt.
- The tips of the leaves will go brown.
- Your plant may start to lose its leaves.
- The growth of your plant will slow down significantly.
- Your plants will die. Seedlings are likely to be affected quicker than mature plants.

If you pick up that you've been slightly overzealous with your fertilizer (it happens to the best of us), all is not necessarily lost. While you may inevitably lose some of your plants (especially younger ones), others can be saved by taking these steps:

- If you can see a fertilizer crust on the surface of your soil, you can carefully remove it using a hand trowel. You can remove the top layer of your soil with the crust, but try your best not to disrupt your plant's root system in the process.
- Leach the fertilizer from your soil with a long, slow watering to flush your plant's roots. This can wash away some of the fertilizer that may have accumulated in your soil. You may have to repeat this a few times.
- Remove any burned or wilted leaves from your plant.
- Carefully mix more good-quality potting soil into your container without disrupting your plant's root system. Alternatively, you can consider repotting your plant, which will increase the risk of stressing your plant.
- Do not fertilize your plant for at least a month after you've treated an overfertilized plant. I would highly recommend that you have your soil tested professionally before you fertilize this plant again, as accidentally overfertilizing the same plant for a second time can be too much for your plant to handle.

A successful garden requires continuous maintenance. This isn't just limited to adding compost and fertilizing your plants and soil; it also includes watering, pruning, staking, and mulching your garden, which we'll discuss in the next chapter.

CHAPTER 9: MAINTENANCE AND CARE

Now that your plants are growing and your garden is thriving, you can turn your focus from starting your garden to maintaining it. This doesn't just mean that you should keep an eye on your soil and your plant's nutritional needs; it also includes watering your garden, pruning away dead buds or leaves, training your plant to grow up a stalk, and choosing the perfect mulch to ensure you give your plant the best possible environment to thrive.

All of these processes can come with challenges. Overwatering can result in your soil flooding, while underwatering can leave your plant to dry out. Pruning your plant at the wrong place can cause dead or infected parts of the plant to stay behind, affecting the overall health of your garden and crops. Using the incorrect trellis for staking your vine plant can result in skewed growth and many other potential problems. Mulching too thickly, especially around your immature plants, can stop their growth altogether.

Luckily, just like you might once have learned how to cook or ride a bicycle, caring for your garden is a skill you can quickly acquire, changing your future for the better. To help you maintain your garden, I will share all the tips and tricks I learned (some the hard way) during my gardening journey.

Watering Your Container Garden

With a traditional in-ground garden or even when your container garden is standing outside, you have the benefit of rain watering your plants. However, if you live in a dry area or if your plants don't get rainwater (either standing under a cover or indoors), giving your plants water will be your responsibility. Even if your garden gets rainwater, it might not be enough. Or, you may stay in such a wet climate that the rainwater might flood your garden and result in root rot. While occasional flooding might not necessarily be detrimental to your garden, permitting your containers to have sufficient drainage holes can severely disrupt your root systems if this happens often.

Let's look at some important factors to keep in mind when it comes to watering your container garden:

- **Know your plants:** The watering needs of different plants can vary quite significantly. For example, lettuce plants are typically very thirsty, while succulents can sometimes go for weeks without a single drop of water. In general, though, juicy vegetables such as tomatoes and cucumbers need a lot of moisture in the soil. Herbs can be more tricky: Some herbs, such as basil, cilantro, dill, oregano, rosemary, and thyme, thrive when their soil dries out between waterings, while others, such as chives, parsley, and sage, want more moisture. As you're planting your crops, I would suggest you make notes of the watering needs of each one so that you can adjust your watering schedule according to your plants' needs.

- **Check moisture levels:** Before you water your garden, you should check how the soil feels to be sure your garden actually needs moisture. This doesn't just mean looking at the soil to see if it appears to be dry: The soil on the surface may be dry to the touch, but underneath, your soil might have sufficient moisture. As a quick test, you can insert your finger into the soil as deeply as possible. If the soil feels dry to your fingertips, you should add water. You should also consider the weather. The soil in your container garden can dry out quickly when it's hot, so even if it has enough moisture in the morning, it may be dry by the afternoon.

- **Water deeply:** Once you've determined that your garden needs water, you might feel unsure of how much water to give it. The answer to this is simply: water deeply until you can see water draining from the holes at the bottom of your container. This is a sign that the water has made it through all the soil in your container, not just the top layer. Doing this will ensure your plant's entire root system has access to water. If you do shallow watering only, your plant's roots won't develop strong systems and will remain near the surface of the soil, where it will be more exposed to drought and heat and won't have access to the nutrients in the soil deeper down in your container.

- **Water your garden early:** It's best to water it in the morning before the sun is at its hottest. This will help your plant absorb water into its roots before evaporation caused by heat and wind takes place. It will also help your plant's leaves to dry out during the day, protecting them from colder temperatures during the night and fungal diseases such as powdery mildew.

- **Water the soil:** Many people make the mistake of simply holding a watering can over their container and dumping the water on top of the plant. The weight of the water can damage your plant's delicate branches and leaves, and, as mentioned above, wet foliage is more susceptible to fungal diseases. Moreover, it won't benefit your plant if the leaves, stems, flowers, or fruits are wet. Plants absorb all their moisture through their roots, so you only have to water the soil, not the plant itself.

- **Don't bank on rain:** Even if your plants receive a lot of rain, they might need additional watering, especially if you have bushy plants. The leaves can act like an umbrella, keeping the rainwater away from your soil and, as a result, the roots. Rainwater is also seldom enough to fully saturate the soil in a large container.

- **Never let your soil dry out:** Unless your specific plant wants to be dry in between waterings, you should never allow your soil to dry out completely. This can affect your soil's ability to absorb water. Also, dry soil often pulls away from the sides of a container, so even if you see water draining at the bottom, it might be from water running down the insides of the container, not saturating the soil. Unfortunately, life happens, and there may be times when you forget to water your garden. If you have a small container that you can easily carry around, you can submerge it in a sink full of water. Only remove the container once the bubbling has stopped, as this is a sign that no air is escaping from the soil. If you have a big container that you can't easily put in a sink, you can use a skewer to gently poke holes in the soil before watering. Repeat this process until the soil is soft and moist.

- **Water more than once:** On very hot and windy days, it may be necessary to water your garden more than once a day. This is often the case with hanging baskets or pots made from terracotta or metal.

Pruning Your Plants

Now, let's turn our attention to pruning, which can be another worrying factor for many newbie gardeners. I remember how awkward I felt when I first had to prune my delicate plants, especially the ones I'd nurtured from seeds. I was so nervous that I was doing it wrong that it took me nearly ten minutes to cut the first branch. Luckily, I soon gained confidence, and now I prune my garden without any hesitation.

Pruning your plants holds many benefits for your garden. If there is any disease or fungus in your plant, pruning the affected leaves and branches will stop it from spreading to healthy leaves and branches. It also helps to improve the spread of sunlight and air circulation around your plant, encouraging fruit production and reducing the spread of disease and fungi.

Here are my three can't-garden-without tips when it comes to pruning:

- **Always cut back:** One of the biggest mistakes I made as a newbie pruner was not cutting the stem, bud, or side branch deep enough. This resulted in unsightly twigs protruding from my plants, but it hampered their growth and fruit development. It's always best to cut back as deep as possible, either to the main stem, a side branch, or a new bud. Since I started doing this, my plants healed quicker when they had diseases, and the quantity of my crops increased drastically.

- **Cut dead or infected parts first:** If you want to prune your garden to increase sunlight and airflow to your plant, it's best to always start with parts of the plant that may be dead or diseased. It often happens that once you've removed the parts of the plants that have seen better days, you don't have to touch any healthy stems, branches, or leaves.

- **Time your pruning:** You don't want to prune your plants when they're about to start producing fruits and vegetables, as you might unknowingly cut off buds where buds might be developing. Instead, use your planting chart and work out when, from planting your crop, you should expect to harvest. Schedule your pruning for a few weeks before you hope to harvest. This will, however, depend on how long your plant takes to develop fruits and vegetables. For annual plants, you can plan your pruning for early spring, as you can then cut off any parts of the plant that might have been negatively affected by the cold winter to make space for new growth during spring.

The Importance of Staking

If you want to grow vegetables like beans or cucumbers, you already know you must stake them. This simply means you'll train your plant to grow up supports so that the vines don't just have space for optimal growth but also so that your crop gets sufficient exposure to the sun and airflow. Again, this might sound easy enough, but my first attempt was a monumental flop. It only took one big gush of wind to destroy my plant, as I not only didn't secure my support properly, but I also didn't use enough plant ties to keep my plant in position. Luckily, I learned many lessons along the way and now have a garden filled with many different supports that aren't just benefiting my plants but also increasing the size of my overall garden; I'm no longer just using the horizontal space I have available for gardening but the vertical space as well.

It might surprise you to hear that not just vining plants benefit from proper staking. Before we go into the details of how to stake your garden, let's look at the different plants that could benefit from staking:

- **Top-heavy plants:** If you have a young plant with a frail stem or weak root system that is top-heavy, you can add support.

This can be something as simple as a bamboo stick to support the stem, especially if you stay in a windy area.

- **Vining plants:** As you probably already know, vining vegetables need staking to boost their crop production. This includes tomatoes, beans, summer squashes, cucumbers, and peas.

- **Wet climate:** If you stay in an area with a lot of rain, fungi can easily spread on your plants. Helping them grow vertically will help protect your plant and crop from fungi.

Choosing the right supports for your plants will largely depend on the type of plant you're growing. As we said, it can be as simple as using a bamboo stick or as intricate as using A-frame cages or fan trellis. However, if you're still building confidence as a gardener, I would suggest you go for a simple grid trellis, as most vegetables do well vining up these. A-frame cages can also be great if you live in a windy area, as they are generally more sturdy than a trellis that simply stands against a wall.

Once you know what plants you want to stake and which support you want to use, let's discuss the "how." If you don't take care to do this properly, your plant might collapse and not only get damaged but also hurt your surrounding plants, as was the case with my first attempt at staking. To help you avoid making the same mistakes, here are my go-to tips:

- **Make sure it's sturdy enough:** You should consider both the type of plant you want to stake, the size it will grow to as it matures, and the typical weather in your area. If you live in a windy area, you should take extra precautions to ensure your support is sturdy. This might mean attaching an upright support to a wall or cementing it into the ground behind your pot.

- **Stake from the start:** You've probably heard the saying, "You can't teach an old dog new tricks." I believe the same can be the case for plants. If you can teach your plant to grow from immaturity, it will grow more successfully and deliver better crops.

- **Make sure your support is smooth:** Young plants can be very delicate, and if you want to stake it onto a rough surface, you might damage your plant and it's soft stems. Also, a thin stem will vine easier on a fine support, which is again why it's so important to consider your plant when deciding on support.

- **Check your plant ties:** When you start staking your plant, you'll use plant ties to encourage their growth in the desired manner. However, many gardeners forget to adjust these ties as the plant matures, which can result in stunting the plant's growth. Continuously check your plant ties and adjust when necessary.

The Benefits of Adding Mulch

I'm sure you've seen many gardens with a layer of wood chips or small pebbles on it, covering the soil. This is called mulch and can make a massive difference to the overall health of your soil and garden. This is due to the many benefits a layer of mulch can bring to your garden, including:

- Reduces the growth of weeds.

- Retains moisture in the soil.

- Control the temperature of the soil so that your plant's roots will stay cooler during warm temperatures and warmer during cold temperatures.

- Reduces disease and fungi growth in your soil.

- Prevents soil compaction.

- Adds nutrients to the garden if organic mulch is used.

As you can see by the last benefit, not all types of mulch will bring your garden the same benefits. Organic mulch, which includes dried grass clippings, pine bark, wood chips, pine needles, straw, and hay, can bring nutrition to your garden as it decomposes. However, it can attract more insects to your garden, and you'll have to replace it frequently, which might not be a problem if you do seasonal planting.

Inorganic mulch, including pebbles, gravel, landscape cloths, and plastic, will provide your garden with long-term protection and won't attract any pests. However, these will also not break down and won't bring any nutrition to your soil. Also, if you plant seasonal plants and you want to reuse your soil after you remove your plants at the end of a season, you'll have to take special care to remove all traces of your inorganic mulch from your soil before you treat it for the next season.

As with most other gardening choices, it's important that you choose the type of mulch that will fit your pocket, garden, and needs. For example, if you plan to grow many bushy types of plants, your mulching needs will be less than if you grow a taller plant where the soil will be more exposed to the elements. Also, remember that dark-colored mulch absorbs heat and may raise soil temperatures. As a result, dark mulch can be ideal during the winter and if you live in a cold climate, while light-colored mulch can be beneficial during the summer or if you stay in a hot area.

If you're planting from seeds, you shouldn't add mulch to your garden until your seedlings are around four inches high. If you add mulch immediately after planting your seeds, your delicate young plants may be too weak to push through the mulch. Once your plant is big enough, you can add around two to three inches of mulch to the top of your soil. You should, however, aim at keeping your mulch around three inches away from the stem of your plant so that your mulch doesn't affect your plant's growth and to avoid any potential disease from spreading. For this reason, you should also ensure none of your plant's leaves touch the mulch. If there is ever any sign of disease in your mulch or if this layer has become too dry to be effective in water retention, you should remove the mulch and add a fresh layer.

Your garden is now set for you to reap the rewards of your hard work. Soon, your first crops will be ready to harvest. In the last chapter, we'll discuss good harvesting techniques as well as recipes and meal ideas to make the most of your crops.

CHAPTER 10: HARVESTING AND ENJOYING YOUR HOMEGROWN BOUNTY

Your garden has grown and developed beautifully, and you see many fruits and vegetables growing and bringing vibrant color to your plants. Soon, you'll be ready to harvest your crops and enjoy your first home-grown meal. This is the time you've been waiting for since you decided to create your container garden.

While some crops are harvested fairly simply by picking your fruits and vegetables, others might be slightly more difficult to harvest. You may also wonder when your crops are ready to be harvested, especially when you're growing root vegetables that you can't see before you remove them from the soil. You might even be surprised to know that, with the right strategies, you can help your crops ripen quicker than they typically would. Once you've harvested your crops, you should also take care of cleaning and storing them properly so that they can last longer than just a day or two, all of which we'll discuss in this final chapter.

Harvesting Your Homegrown Bounty

Harvesting your crops is one of the most rewarding parts of gardening. You'll soon be able to enjoy the fruits of your efforts. But before you can start preparing your first home-grown meal, you need to get your bounty from your garden to your kitchen. This is where harvesting comes in. Ensure you have all the right tools for the task before starting. This includes sharp scissors or pruners, a clean container where you can put your harvested produce, and wipes or soap to clean your tools not just while you're busy but also after you're done. Also, make sure your hands are cleaned thoroughly before you start to prevent potentially bringing disease to your garden.

I suggest you try to harvest your crops early in the day while it's cooler than in the midday sun. This will ensure that your bounty is well-hydrated when you pick them. Also, don't harvest when it's raining, as disease and fungi spread more easily in wet weather, and since you'll touch many of your plants, you must protect your garden at all times. Check your crops properly after harvest for any signs of bruises, animals damage, or contamination from animal or bird droppings.

Keep these products away from your healthy ones to prevent disease or contamination from spreading. Unless there are signs of disease, these damaged crops can be used for composting. Handle your healthy produce carefully to avoid damaging them. Keep your harvested crops in the shade to reduce moisture loss.

Just like most other gardeners, I've developed my own tricks to make harvesting and caring for my crops a lot easier and even quicker, which I'll now share with you:

- **Promote repeat cropping:** While some vegetable plants will only give you a single harvest in a season, many others can give a second crop, albeit smaller, if you leave the plant in the soil after the main harvest. For example, simply cut the broccoli or cabbage heads off or slice your leafy greens from the outside while keeping the stem and roots intact. Continue watering your garden as usual.

- **Harvesting your root crops:** Removing root crops from the soil can require some serious pulling and muscle flexing. Using a hand cultivator to loosen the soil around the vegetable, it will pull out a lot easier. When you pull a root vegetable, don't work on pulling it straight out. Instead, grab the crop by the stem and gently rock it back and forth to loosen it until it comes out.

- **Clean your vegetables:** Once you've harvested your bounty, you should clean them to remove any dirt and debris. If you do this one by one, you'll spend a lot of time on it. Instead, you can put your crop in a mesh container, such as a plastic laundry basket, inside a bucket filled with water to clean. When you're done, you can use the muddy water for your growing garden to avoid messing up a drop.

- **Brush it off:** Some vegetables, such as root vegetables like potatoes, shouldn't be submerged in water. Instead, you can simply leave them out for a few minutes to dry. Then, use your fingers, a dry cloth, or even a toothbrush to remove excess dirt.

- **Trick the birds:** There's nothing more frustrating than to see animals such as birds eat your beautiful crops. Luckily, I found a way to outsmart these birds: Christmas baubles. Simply hang these colorful baubles between your ripening fruits and vegetables. Birds will be attracted to your baubles, and when pecking at them won't give them any results, they will move on.

If you plan to store your harvests for later use, you can wrap your produce in either a paper or cloth towel and place it in the fridge. If you want to store your harvested vegetables like peppers, onions, and tomatoes, it's best not to wash them immediately after you pick them. Instead, brush the excess dirt off them and wash them only before you want to eat them. This will help them last longer in your fridge.

Identifying Your Ripe Harvests

With some fruits and vegetables, you can clearly see when they are ripe enough to be harvested. For example, tomatoes should be red and soft to the touch, while broccoli will have a perfect head visible. With other crops, it can be more difficult to know when it's time to pull up, pluck, or pick your crops. Over the years and with the wide variety of crops I've grown, I've found many tricks to help me know when to harvest:

- **Root crops**
    - The size of your carrots will depend on the container you use to grow them. However, you'll know they are edible when the tops have turned into a bright orange. The fun thing with carrots is that you can leave them in the soil and only harvest them as you use them.
    - A tell-tale sign that parsnips are ready is when the foliage starts to die back.
    - Beets can be plucked at any size, so once you're leaves have developed properly, you can pull one out to see. If you want to pickle your beets, you can pick them at around golf ball size. If you want bigger beets, leave them in the soil longer.

- **Potatoes**

    - Your potatoes should be ready for harvesting once the plants develop flowers, which is usually around 10 to 12 weeks from planting. To check the size of your crops, you can gently scratch the soil from the sides of your containers to expose the top of a potato.

    - If you want to grow maincrop potatoes, you should only harvest your crops after the leaves have died back, which is usually around 20 weeks from planting.

    - Beans and peas

    - You can check if your broad beans and peas are ready for harvesting by gripping their pods gently. This will allow you to feel the size of the vegetables growing inside them.

    - With climbing beans, the pods should be smooth and long, without necessarily seeing beans bulging inside them.

- **Fruiting vegetables**

    - With vegetables like tomatoes and peppers, you can look at the color of the skin and the softness of the touch. Make sure the entire vegetable has an even color before you pick them.

    - A sign that your cucumbers are ready is when the vegetable no longer has a pronounced point at the tip.

    - Zucchini squash can be picked once they are around four inches long.

- **Salad leaves**

    - On loose-leaf salad greens, you can harvest as soon as the leaves are big enough to enjoy. Harvest your outer leaves first, as this will allow the inner leaves to continue growing.

  - With heart-forming lettuce, you can harvest as soon as the heart has started to firm up.

- **Cabbage, broccoli, and cauliflower**

  - You can harvest your cabbages once the leaves have developed a firm, tight head.
  - Flowering plants like broccoli or cauliflower can be picked once a head has formed but ideally while the buds are still closed.

- **Garlic and onions**

  - Your garlic and onions are ready for harvesting once the leaves start to die back. If you want to keep your garlic and onions, you can leave them in the soil for an extra week or two until the leaves have turned yellow.

- **Tree fruits**

  - Look at the color and size of your tree fruits to determine when they are ready for picking. For softer fruits, such as nectarines and peaches, you can gently feel the stalk side of the fruit. If it's slightly soft to the touch, they are ready.

- **Soft fruits**

  - Currants and berries should be an even color when they're ripe. Blackcurrants should be left for around a week after turning black to be full of flavor, while blueberries should be left for around three days after turning blue for proper flavor development. When you pick your fluffy and soft strawberries, ensure the cap remains attached to the fruit.

- **Herbs**
    - You can harvest your herbs once the leaves are fragrant and thick, ideally before flowering, as this is when the foliage will have the most flavor.

Ripen Your Harvests Quicker

There may be times when you want to rush your crops to ripen quicker. This is often when you're starting your garden and eager to reap the rewards of your first bounty, or when you're nearing the end of your growing season and fear your crops won't be ready before the first frost sets in. If you can bring your containers indoors, ripening your crops before the end of the season might not be a big concern, but if your garden is permanently outside, there are many tricks you can do to speed up the ripening of your crops. When I first heard about ripening your harvests, I honestly thought many of these suggestions were old wives' tales that wouldn't really work. After trying them, I was both surprised and impressed. Here are the techniques that I found work best:

- This one was probably the most bizarre of all the techniques I tried, but tomatoes can ripen quicker if you stress the plant. You can do this by reducing the amount of water you give it or disturbing the roots slightly by repeatedly cutting a semicircle around the plant's stem using a hand trowel or cultivator. You can even yank on the stem to disrupt the root system without breaking the roots completely.

- Flowering vegetables like peppers and chili plants will produce many vegetables over the course of a season. The more you harvest, the quicker your plants will produce more crops. If you want to rush this, you can start to pick your crops as soon as they are almost ripe or even prune away new buds that might form so that the plant can focus its energy on completing the development of the other crops.

- You can place your hard fruit in a paper bag loosely closed at the top to trap the ethylene gas from the fruit in the bag and quicken the ripening process. Adding big ethylene producers like bananas or apples in the bag can boost this even more. Another way to trap the ethylene from fruits is by submerging them in a bowl of uncooked rice.

- Delicate fruits like nectarines or peaches can be placed stem-down between two layers of breathable linen, such as a muslin cloth.

Always remember that any produce that isn't getting ripe or spoiled after you forgot to harvest in time can be used in your compost bin to create food for your soil to boost your future bounty. No part of your garden should ever go to waste!

CONCLUSION

Container gardening isn't just about nurturing plants; it's a journey filled with rewards, growth, and an absolutely delicious home-grown bounty. The beauty of container gardening is its versatility. Limited space doesn't limit possibilities. Instead, it fuels creativity. I found myself experimenting with different containers, exploring vertical gardening solutions, and discovering the adaptability of plants to thrive in confined spaces.

Reflecting on my container gardening experience, I'm amazed by the bountiful harvests, the joy of nurturing life, and the satisfaction of savoring homegrown goodness. My journey into container gardening began with a simple desire for fresh herbs. Little did I know it would evolve into a profound connection with nature and a source of both relaxation and empowerment. Tending to my containers, from herbs to vegetables, became a ritual: a therapeutic escape from daily stresses and a mindful engagement with the earth.

What began as a modest attempt soon revealed the immense impact of container gardening. Not only did I relish the vibrant flavors of freshly picked produce, but I also felt a profound sense of accomplishment and self-sufficiency. With each successful harvest, I grew more determined to expand my garden oasis.

My journey has taught me about the inherent environmental and health benefits of organic gardening. Embracing organic practices isn't just a trend; it's a commitment to sustainability and well-being. Knowing that my produce is free from harmful chemicals brings me a lot of peace of mind, while reducing my carbon footprint, which feels like a small but impactful contribution to our planet.

Beyond the tangible rewards, container gardening reshaped my lifestyle. It encouraged healthier eating habits, inspiring me to incorporate more fresh produce into my meals. The satisfaction of sharing homegrown herbs and vegetables with friends and family sparked conversations about sustainable living and the joys of gardening.

I encourage anyone considering container gardening to take that leap. Start small, perhaps with a few herbs or a compact vegetable. Witness the magic of growth and be prepared for a journey that transcends the boundaries of a physical garden. It's about nurturing plants and a sense of connection, mindfulness, and well-being. Remember, container gardening isn't just about what you grow; it's about the values you cultivate—the appreciation for nature's cycles, the commitment to sustainable practices, and the joy of reaping what you sow, both in your garden and in life.

Now, it's your turn. It's up to you to bring the same level of peace to nature while enjoying organic produce straight from your home. It's your turn to improve your holistic health and well-being by not only enjoying your organic bounty but also using your gardening journey as an amazing stress-relieving practice. Believe in yourself and the green fingers you'll develop through your journey. You can do it!

Did You Enjoy This Book? Please Leave a Review!

I write because I have a passion for self-improvement. Feedback from my readers inspires me and helps me to improve as both an author and a trainer. If you enjoyed this book, please leave a review on Amazon. It would mean a lot to me to know what you think!

BONUS CHAPTER: REVIVING LEFTOVERS: REGROWING FOOD FROM KITCHEN SCRAPS

Before starting my first garden, I had no issue throwing away food scraps or even vegetables that were forgotten in the back of the fridge. I had the philosophy that if I wasn't going to eat it, it had no place in my home. Everything changed once I successfully grew my first vegetables. I started to view nature completely differently and appreciated every inch of every vegetable I harvested, so much so that I refused to throw anything out.

I first started to repurpose my kitchen scraps to make compost. This provided me with buckets full of black gold to fuel my garden. Then I ventured into a whole new form of gardening: regrowing new vegetable plants from scraps. At first, I was surprised at how many vegetables you can grow from the scraps that usually end up in the dust bin or the compost pile.

Apart from feeling like I'm creating another small victory for the environment and continuously having new plants to produce more harvests, I also saved a lot of money, as I didn't have to buy as many seeds or seedlings to keep my garden going. I even saved on my refuse removal bill, as my kitchen waste drastically decreased. What an unexpected bonus!

Step-by-Step Guide to Regrow Your Vegetables

Let's now look at the steps you can take to regrow some of the most popular vegetables and herbs from the scraps you would typically throw away. In most cases, you don't need specialized equipment to repurpose your waste in this organically wonderful way. A shallow tray with water, your potting soil, and a warm windowsill are usually all it takes.

Some of these vegetables and fruits can take some time to redevelop from the scraps (I've given up on growing an avocado tree from the pip), while others redevelop surprisingly quickly into beautiful young plants. Here are some of my absolute favorites:

- **Basil, cilantro, mint, and many other herbs:** There are many herbs that can easily regrow from plant cuttings or scraps. Take a leafy stem from these herbs (it should be around four inches long) and place it in a glass of water. Make sure that the leaves don't touch the water. Within a few days, you'll see new roots developing. Once these roots are big enough, you can plant them in the soil.

- **Broccoli, cabbages, and cauliflower:** The next time you prepare these vegetables, try to keep as much of the stem part of the head intact. Place this in a shallow water dish on a sunny windowsill and keep it moist. Within a few weeks, you'll see an entire new root system that you can plant in the soil. Alternatively, when you harvest broccoli, cabbages, or cauliflower from your garden, you can cut a cross in the base of the remaining stem in your garden. More often than not, a second head will start to develop.

- **Carrots, beets, radishes, and other root vegetables:** Take the top of the vegetable (the section where the leaves and stems join to the vegetable) and place it face down in a shallow water container. New green tops will start growing from the vegetables within a few days. Leave this for another couple of days for new roots to develop before you plant them in your soil.

- **Celery:** I found celery to be one of the plants that regrows the easiest from scraps. Just cut off the bottom of the celery bunch and place it in warm water in a shallow container. Place this on a warm windowsill. Within a week or so, your celery bottoms will now be full of leaves you can harvest directly or plant in your soil.

- **Fennel:** This herb regrows in pretty much the same way as celery does. Simply place the base of the fennel bulb in shallow water for it to regrow. If your bulb still has some roots attached to it, you'll see the new green shoots emerge even faster. Once sufficient new shoots are on your bulb, you can plant it in your container to grow a new plant.

- **Garlic and onions:** These can easily be regrown from the rooting base of the bulb or the stem. It's best to leave some of the original roots on the bulb or stem. Simply place this in a shallow dish of water. In less than a week, you'll see green sprouts forming. These can then be harvested and planted directly in your soil.

- **Lettuce and other leafy greens:** Leafy greens are the plants that keep giving. Throughout a season, you can cut leaves as you need them, and they will continue to grow back. However, any head-forming leafy green can be regrown from kitchen scraps. Simply put the scraps of the head (that hard part where the stem grows) in water and wait for new leaves to grow. If you keep this in a sunny spot in your home and keep it moist with a water sprayer, new roots will begin to form on your head, which you can then plant in your soil.

- **Potatoes:** A potato's skin is filled with tiny indentations or spots called the "eye" of the potato. This is where the shoots grow, from which they will form new plants. If you've left potatoes for too long, you might have seen this process start in your kitchen. The next time shoots start to grow in the kitchen, or you peel a potato, don't discard it. Instead, let the peels dry out slightly overnight, and then you can place them with the eye showing upwards straight into your soil. Water it well, and soon, you'll see new potato plants sprouting.

- **Sweet potato:** If you have left a sweet potato for too long to eat, you can use it to grow a new plant. Simply cut the vegetable in half, push a few toothpicks into it, and let it hang suspended over a water container. A mason jar works well for this. Put this on a warm windowsill. Within a few days, you'll see tiny roots developing from your sweet potato, turning into sprouts. Once these sprouts are around four inches long, you can cut them off and place them base down in a container of water. Within a few days, roots will grow from these sprouts, which you can then plant in the soil.

References

Bartholomew, M. (n.d.). *Planting chart cheat sheets.* Square Foot Gardening. https://squarefootgardening.org/planting-chart-cheat-sheets/

Best soil options for container gardening - explained. (2022, January 6). Gardening Channel. https://www.gardeningchannel.com/best-soil-container-gardening/

Boeckmann, C. (2024, March 14). *Tips for transplanting seedlings outdoors in the garden.* Old Farmer's Almanac. https://www.almanac.com/tips-transplanting-seedlings

Carlson, C. (2024, May 21). *Vegetable planting calendar.* University of Maryland Extension. https://extension.umd.edu/resource/vegetable-planting-calendar/

Carr, R. (2016, January 6). *Vermicomposting for beginners.* Rodale Institute. https://rodaleinstitute.org/science/articles/vermicomposting-for-beginners/

Container gardening. (n.d.). School Gardening. https://schoolgardening.rhs.org.uk/resources/info-sheet/container-gardening

Gonzalez, R. (2018, October 11). *Test your potting soil quality before planting your container garden.* Treehugger. https://www.treehugger.com/test-your-potting-soil-quality-soil-planting-your-container-garden-4857230

Gopi. (2019, March 2). *10 essential container gardening tools.* Pinch of Seeds. https://pinchofseeds.com/container-gardening-tools/

Greener Ideal Staff. (2023, November 29). *How to make your own neem oil pesticide.* Greener Ideal. https://greenerideal.com/guides/0814-how-to-make-your-own-neem-oil-pesticide/

Guide to trellising and staking in your gardens. (2023, May 2). All That Grows. https://www.allthatgrows.in/blogs/posts/trellis-stake-garden-plant-supports

Iannotti, M. (2021, November 8). *Identifying plant pests and diseases.* The Spruce. https://www.thespruce.com/insects-and-diseases-of-plants-4070266

Leverette, M. M. (2024, February 10). *Vegetable container gardening for beginners.* The Spruce. https://www.thespruce.com/vegetable-container-gardening-for-beginners-848161

Michaels, K. (2024, April 26). *10 tips on how to water your container gardens.* The Spruce. https://www.thespruce.com/watering-plants-in-containers-847785

Mowinski, D. (2020, October 8). *Pruning container trees and shrubs: 5 tips.* Urban Turnip. https://www.urbanturnip.org/pruning-container-trees-and-shrubs-5-tips/

Pelczar, R. (2024, February 20). *8 common composting mistakes you might be making (and how to fix them).* Better Homes & Gardens. https://www.bhg.com/gardening/yard/compost/9-common-composting-mistakes-you-may-be-making/

Reich, L. (2014, April 25). *A secret recipe for great homemade potting soil.* FineGardening. https://www.finegardening.com/project-guides/container-gardening/soil-in-containers-should-be-a-good-mix

Seeds vs. seedlings: what is better? (2017, February 17). Hortidaily. https://www.hortidaily.com/article/6032426/seeds-vs-seedlings-what-is-better/

Sweetser, R. (2024a, April 8). *DIY potting soil recipe to save money.* Almanac. https://www.almanac.com/how-make-your-own-potting-mix

Sweetser, R. (2024b, April 26). *Testing soil pH and soil health (right at home!).* Old Farmer's Almanac. https://www.almanac.com/content/3-simple-diy-soil-tests

Sweetser, R. (2024c, May 13). *Vegetable container gardening for beginners.* Old Farmer's Almanac. https://www.almanac.com/content/container-gardening-vegetables

The Editors of Good Housekeeping. (2018, August 13). *Everything you need to know about container gardening.* Good Housekeeping. https://www.goodhousekeeping.com/home/gardening/a20707074/container-gardening-tips/

The ultimate guide to seasonal gardening. (2017, December 5). Garden Goods Direct. https://gardengoodsdirect.com/blogs/news/ultimate-guide-to-seasonal-gardening

Trail, G. (2024, May 6). *How to make organic plant fertilizer at home.* Old Farmer's Almanac. https://www.almanac.com/how-make-organic-plant-fertilizer-home

Vanheems, B. (2017, August 11). *How to tell when fruits and vegetables are ready for harvest.* GrowVeg. https://www.growveg.co.za/guides/how-to-tell-when-fruits-and-vegetables-are-ready-for-harvest/

Vanheems, B. (2018, August 29). *6 ways to extend your harvests.* GrowVeg. https://www.growveg.co.za/guides/6-ways-to-extend-your-harvests/

Vanheems, B. (2024, April 24). *Best companion plants for tomatoes, potatoes, peppers, beans, & more.* Almanac. https://www.almanac.com/companion-planting-guide-vegetables

Waddington, E. (2019, November 14). *20 vegetables you can regrow from scraps.* Rural Sprout. https://www.ruralsprout.com/regrow-vegetables/

What is compost? (n.d.). Planet Natural Research Center. https://www.planetnatural.com/composting-101/soil-science/what-is-compost/

Made in the USA
Monee, IL
05 March 2025